C000246979

GCSE History

Germany 1918–1945

Second Edition

Aaron Wilkes

OXFORD

UNIVERSITY PRESS

OXFORD
UNIVERSITY PRESS

Great Clarendon Street, Oxford OX2 6DP

Oxford University Press is a department of the University of Oxford.
It furthers the University's objective of excellence in research,
scholarship, and education by publishing worldwide in

Oxford   New York

Auckland   Cape Town   Dar es Salaam   Hong Kong   Karachi
Kuala Lumpur   Madrid   Melbourne   Mexico City   Nairobi
New Delhi   Shanghai   Taipei   Toronto

With offices in

Argentina   Austria   Brazil   Chile   Czech Republic   France   Greece
Guatemala   Hungary   Italy   Japan   Poland   Portugal   Singapore
South Korea   Switzerland   Thailand   Turkey   Ukraine   Vietnam

Oxford is a registered trade mark of Oxford University Press
in the UK and in certain other countries

© Aaron Wilkes 2009

The moral rights of the author have been asserted

Database right Oxford University Press (maker)

First published 2009

All rights reserved. No part of this publication may be reproduced,
stored in a retrieval system, or transmitted, in any form or by any means,
without the prior permission in writing of Oxford University Press, or as
expressly permitted by law, or under terms agreed with the appropriate
reprographics rights organization. Enquiries concerning reproduction
outside the scope of the above should be sent to the Rights Department,
Oxford University Press, at the address above

You must not circulate this book in any other binding or cover
and you must impose this same condition on any acquirer

British Library Cataloguing in Publication Data

Data available

ISBN 978-1-85008-459-4

FD4594

10 9 8 7 6 5 4 3 2

Printed in Singapore by KHL Printing Co Pte Ltd

Paper used in the production of this book is a natural, recyclable product
made from wood grown in sustainable forests. The manufacturing process
conforms to the environmental regulations of the country of origin.

Author's acknowledgements

The author wishes to thank Kate Greig for her hard work and
patience. He would also like to acknowledge the help and
support of Emma Wilkes during the preparation of this book.

Series design: Neil Sutton, Pumpkin House, Cambridge

Text design and layout: Neil Sutton, Pumpkin House
Cambridge

Picture researcher: Sue Sharp

Illustrators: Neil Sutton (pages 8, 22, 23 and 91); Jim
Eldridge, Beehive

Cover design: Richard Jervis Design

Front Cover image: © Selecta/Alamy

Photo acknowledgements

p.5 © Hulton-Collection/CORBIS; pp.6–7 © Ullstein-Archiv
Gerstenberg; p.8 © Topfoto; p.9 Getty Images; p.16 (top)
Bettmann/CORBIS; p.16 (bottom) Aaron Wilkes; p.18 ©
Bettmann/CORBIS; p.19 (left) © CORBIS, (right) AFP/Getty Images;
p.20 © Hulton-Deutsch Collection/CORBIS; p.24 © Ullstein Bild; p.26
© Austrian Archives/CORBIS; p.29 akg-images, London; p.33 Imperial
War Museum; p.36 Time & Life Pictures/Getty Images; p.38
Grosstadt' (urban debauchery) 1927–28 (triptych) (oil on canvas),
Dix, Otto (1891–1969) /Staatsgalerie, Stuttgart, Germany/Bridgeman
Art Library, copyright DACS' visual creators for the use of their artistic
works / © DACS 2009; p.39 Sidney George Strube, published in the
Daily Express 7th May 1919/Centre for the Study of Cartoons and
Caricature, University of Kent; p.45 © CORBIS; p.47 Time & Life
Pictures/Getty Images; p.48 © Hulton-Deutsch Collection/CORBIS;
p.50 (left) akg-images, London, (right) Getty Images; p.51 (left) ©
Bettmann/CORBIS, (right) Bayerische Staatsbibliothek/Bavarian State
Library, Munich; p.53 © Bettmann/CORBIS; p.54 USHMM, coutesy of
Andras Tsagatakis; p.59 © Hulton-Deutsch Collection/CORBIS; p.61
MARY EVANS/WEIMAR ARCHIVE; p.62 © CORBIS; p.64 akg-images,
London; p.66 Robert Hunt Library/Mary Evans Picture Library; p.67
© Hulton-Deutsch Collection/CORBIS; p.72 © Bettmann/CORBIS;
p.73 (top) © Hulton-Deutsch Collection/CORBIS, (bottom) ©
Bettmann/CORBIS; p.74 Time & Life Pictures/Getty Images; p.75 ©
CORBIS; p.76 MARY EVANS/WEIMAR ARCHIVE; p.83 (left) Time &
Life Pictures/Getty Images, (right) © Ullstein Bild; p.84 Mary Evans
Picture Library; p.87 © Hulton-Deutsch Collection/CORBIS; pp.88–9
Everett Collection/Rex Features; p.91 Suddeutscher Verlag
Bilderdienst; p.92 Suddeutscher Verlag Bilderdienst; p.93 © Ullstein
Bild; p.94 © Gianni Giansanti/Sygma/Corbis; p.95 (top) Mary Evans
Picture Library, (bottom) © CORBIS; p.97 © Bettmann/CORBIS; p.100
Time & Life Pictures/Getty Images; p.101 Getty Images; p.102 Solo
Syndication/Associated Newspapers Ltd; p.103 © MILNER
MOSHE/CORBIS SYGMA.

Text acknowledgements

pp.4 (bottom left and right), 17 *Weimar Germany* by Josh Brooman,
Longman (1985); pp.11, 29, 31 BBC *History File: Nazi Germany
Episode One*; p.13 BBC *1919: Lost Peace: People's Century*, 1997; p.18,
49 (top right) *The Twentieth Century* by J.D. Clare, Nelson Thornes
(1993); p.30, 31 BBC *The Nazis: A Warning from History*; p.45, 100
(right) *Hitler's Germany* by Josh Brooman, Longman (1985); pp.49
(bottom left) *Nazi Power in Germany* by Greg Thie and Jean Thie,
Nelson Thornes (1991); p.51 *Inside the Third Reich* by Albert Speer,
Weidenfeld & Nicholson (2003); p.57 *GCSE Modern World History* by
Ben Walsh, John Murray (1996); p.68 *In Hitler's Germany* by Bernt
Engelmann, Methuen (1988); p.69 *The War Path* by David Irving,
Focal Point Publications (1978); p.91 BBC History File: *Nazi Germany
Episode Two*; p.96 *The Memoirs of the SS Kommandant at Auschwitz* by
Rudolf Höss, Da Capo Press (1996).

Some of the exam questions have been taken from the OCR (formerly
MEG) examination papers from 1988–2005.

The wording and sentence structure of some written sources have
been adapted and simplified to make them accessible to all students,
while faithfully preserving the sense of the original.

Contents

Germany and the Great War

Topic Focus

▸ To understand at least two difficulties faced by ordinary Germans during the Great War.
▸ To know why the German emperor ran away to Holland.

Exam Focus

▸ What impact did the Great War have on Germany and its citizens?

The Great War began in August 1914 when seven countries went to war with each other – Germans and Austrians against the French, British, Russians, Belgians and Serbs. Over the next four years, dozens of countries would join in.

When war first broke out, it had been very popular in Germany. Like most men all over Europe, young Germans thought the war would be great fun, a chance to lead daring attacks, shoot guns, capture prisoners and win medals. Instead, the war turned into a nightmare for the soldiers – they were pounded by bombs, poisoned by gas or cut down by machine gun fire. Even in Germany, women, children and old people began to suffer too. So what were conditions really like in Germany during the war? How did these problems lead to revolution? And why exactly did the Great War end at 11:00am on 11 November 1918?

It did not take long for people in Germany to start suffering during the war. The British had a huge navy and decided to use it to stop supply ships getting to Germany throughout the war. If a ship taking food into Germany was spotted by a British ship, it would be asked to turn around … or be blown up! As a result, there were terrible food shortages in Germany from as early as 1915 (see **Sources B** and **C**).

▾ **Source A** *A young man's thoughts on hearing that Germany had joined the Great War. This particular soldier went on to fight very bravely throughout the war – his name was Adolf Hitler.*

"I am not ashamed to admit today that I was carried away by the enthusiasm of the moment. I sank down on my knees and thanked heaven for having been allowed to live at such a time."

▾ **Source B** *A description of conditions in Germany.*

"…the average adult German was living on 1000 calories a day – half the amount needed for a normal healthy diet. Coal was running short and, because gas and electricity were made from coal, there were power cuts as well. In many cities, all public buildings, cinemas and theatres were closed down. Lights in apartment blocks were put out early."

▾ **Source C** *An Australian woman, living in Berlin during the war, writing to her sister. Germany's potato crop was destroyed by frost in the winter of 1916. Most people lived on turnips instead! Even in Germany today, this period of history is known as the 'turnip winter'.*

"My dear Emmie,

We have got through a strange week – the worst week the German people has had to face up to the present. No coal, electric light turned off, the gas power turned down … and practically no food – there seems to be no more potatoes – each of us has been given half a pound of what they call potato-flocken. I know no English word for it – they seem to me to be the dried skins of potatoes – you have to soak them overnight, then rub them through a sieve…. We had a half pound of that, five pounds of turnips, 3 ^{1}/2 pounds of bread, and that was all. I went the rounds of the restaurants and sometimes got some cabbage, or a tiny piece of chicken that cost 3/– [3 shillings] or edible toadstools, and I bought tinned fish at 5/– a pound, but it passes my understanding to know how the poor are managing. Any other people on earth would rise against a government that had reduced it to such misery, but these folk seem to have no spirit left….

Very much love to you all,

From your loving Ethel."

▼ **Source D** *German children surround a street soup kitchen in 1918.*

FACT *'flu*

During 1918, a killer virus called Spanish Influenza (or 'flu) swept across Europe. It killed an estimated 30 million people in total. In Germany, the years of hunger and dirt (there were shortages of soap and washing powder too) took their toll – nearly half a million German civilians and 200 000 German soldiers died in the summer of 1918.

TOP EXAM TIP

The word 'impact' is used a lot in exam questions. Make sure you know what it means ... and practice exam questions with the word 'impact' in! For example, 'What was the impact of the Great War on Germany?'

As the war continued, there were demands in Germany for peace. In 1915, 500 women gathered in front of the German parliament buildings and said that they wanted their men back from the trenches. A year later, 10 000 workers assembled in Berlin's city centre to shout 'Down with war, down with the government'. The police quickly moved in to make arrests!

By the beginning of 1918, Germany was close to collapse. Early protests against food shortages by some had turned into a complete refusal to support the war at all by many. Even some soldiers had refused to fight! In August 1918, as Germany entered its fourth year of war, it seemed as if most German citizens were desperate for the war to end.

In October 1918, General Ludendorff, a leading army general, told shocked German politicians that they could never win the war. He thought Germany should 'abandon the war as hopeless' and advised that the British, French and Americans would perhaps treat Germany more fairly if they stopped fighting soon. However, ending the war wasn't a decision the politicians could make – it was Germany's emperor, Kaiser Wilhelm's choice. So did he decide to continue fighting or take advice from one of his best soldiers and ask for a ceasefire? The Kaiser decided to fight on!

On 28 October, the German navy, based in Kiel, was ordered out to sea to attack British ships. Sailors on the ships refused to follow orders – they just didn't want to fight any more. News of their **mutiny** began to spread. In ports nearby, other sailors refused to follow orders. Along with workers and soldiers, they began to take over towns and set up special councils to run them. In just six days, workers' and soldiers' councils were governing cities all over Germany, like Hamburg and Munich. The country was in chaos and there was little the Kaiser could do – he had lost control and his army generals refused to help him. On 9 November 1918, he **abdicated** and secretly left Germany by tram. He went to live in Holland, never to return.

Friedrich Ebert, one of the leaders of Germany's largest political party, took the Kaiser's place as leader of Germany on a temporary basis. He promised to hold elections soon. If ordinary German people wanted him as their leader, they would get the chance to vote for him if they wished. Meanwhile, he gave the people what they really wanted – an end to the war. On 11 November, at 11:00am, Germany surrendered. The Great War was over. Germans today call the chaos of October and November the "German Revolution of 1918".

▶ **Source E** *A photograph taken during the revolution in Berlin in the first week of November 1918. It shows soldiers and workers riding around the streets on a stolen lorry. Note the machine gun attached to the lorry's roof.*

FACT *The Kaiser: brave or stupid?*

In early 1918, the Kaiser sent a relative, Prince Max, to talk to the American President about ending the war. President Woodrow Wilson told him that the Kaiser must give up some of his power and the Reichstag, Germany's parliament, must have a greater say in the running of the country. The Kaiser refused to make any changes ... and the war continued.

FACT *Germany stands alone*

By 1918, Germany's only allies were Bulgaria, Austria-Hungary and Turkey. By 4 November, they had all surrendered, leaving Germany to fight on alone.

▼ **Source F** *Adapted from a list of demands from a workers' council in 1918. It gives you an idea of how Kaiser Wilhelm had limited the freedom of ordinary German citizens over the years.*

We want:

i) peace;

ii) increased supplies of food;

iii) the right to free speech;

iv) the right to hold public meetings;

v) the right to form trade unions;

vi) the release of all political prisoners;

vii) the introduction of general, equal and secret voting for all men and women over 20 years of age.

▼ **Source G** *Not all soldiers were happy that the war was over. This soldier wrote down his memories at the end of the war whilst he was injured in hospital. His name was Adolf Hitler.*

"Tension increased in November. Then disaster came. Sailors arrived in lorries and told us to revolt. A few Jewish youths were the leaders but not one of them had been to the front to fight. The rumours grew more and more definite — what I had thought to be a local affair was apparently a countrywide revolution. On top of this, distressing news came back from the front. They wanted to surrender. Yes — was such a thing possible? The sacrifices and suffering, the starvation and thirst for many months, the hours doing our duty, gripped by fear, the death of two million men — had they died for this, so that a gang of miserable criminals could lay hands on the fatherland?"

WISE UP WORDS

- mutiny   abdicate

WORK

1 **a** Make a list of the ways in which conditions in Germany got worse from 1914 to 1918.

   b Give two reasons why the war caused such bad conditions for ordinary Germans.

2 Look at **Source C**. How can you tell from Ethel's letter that conditions in Germany were far worse for many other people than they were for her?

3 Look at **Source D**.

   a Why do you think these children were queuing for food?

   b Do you think that the children pictured here came from richer or poorer German families? Give a reason for your answer.

4 **a** Explain what is meant by the word 'abdicate'.

   b In your own words, explain why Germany's emperor, Kaiser Wilhelm, decided to abdicate.

5 Look at **Source F**.

   Does this source help explain why many ordinary Germans were so keen to get rid of Kaiser Wilhelm? Explain your answers carefully.

6 Look at **Source G**.

   What does this source tell us about Hitler's feelings at the end of the war?

What was the Weimar Republic?

Topic Focus

▸ The next four pages give you background information on what happened to Germany after the Great War. They will help you understand how the Weimar Republic got its name and how it was governed.

Exam Focus

▸ Identify at least two problems that the Weimar Republic faced.

Kaiser Wilhelm II had been Germany's emperor since 1888. Despite having help from a parliament, (or Reichstag, which was elected by the people), it was the Kaiser who introduced laws, selected the men for important government jobs, declared war and made peace. He only allowed his Reichstag to change laws occasionally. There were a number of different political parties in the Reichstag but the Kaiser took none of them very seriously. In fact, he once called the politicians in the Reichstag 'a troop of monkeys, blockheads and sleepwalkers'. In short, Kaiser Wilhelm was a **dictator** with complete power.

So how would Germany cope now the Kaiser had run off to Holland? Who would lead the country and how would it be ruled? And would all Germans be happy with their new leader?

▾ **Source A** *Friedrich Ebert.*

The Kaiser left Germany on 9 November 1918. He had taken the country into a war of which many Germans were now thoroughly sick and tired. There were riots and rebellions all over Germany as millions of people grew close to starvation. Friedrich Ebert, the leader of the largest political party in the country, took the Kaiser's place as leader of Germany. On 11 November, Germany surrendered, bringing an end to a much-hated war. Next, Ebert ordered improvements to living conditions – a shorter working day, help for the unemployed, better housing and more food supplies. He guaranteed freedom of speech, freedom of religion and arranged elections for a new German parliament. He declared that Germany would be a **democratic republic** from now on – there would be no Kaiser or emperor; instead, ordinary Germans could choose their leaders by voting for them.

To many, it sounded like Ebert was the sort of leader who might do a good job. His actions so far seemed to show he cared about the citizens of Germany. But not everyone was pleased. A group of **Communists** (see Information box 1), known as the Spartacus League, wanted Germany to be run by soldiers' and workers' councils, not by a parliament. They wanted Germany to be a Communist country, like Russia, and tried to start another revolution in January 1919. Thousands of Spartacists (as they were known) roamed around the streets of Berlin firing guns and taking over important buildings. Ebert responded with a violent solution – he sent in a group of 2000 tough ex-soldiers known as the **Free Corps** to attack the Spartacists (see Information box 2). After three days of brutal street fighting, the Free Corps recaptured buildings and arrested Rosa Luxemburg and Karl Liebknecht, the leaders of the Spartacus League. After beating them savagely, the Free Corps shot them and dumped their dead bodies in the street. The Spartacus League's revolt was over.

Now Ebert held the election that he had promised. His own political party, the Social Democrats, won the most votes and Ebert became the new German President. Because of all the recent violence in Berlin, the newly elected politicians, with Ebert as President, met up on 11 February 1919 in a town in southern Germany called Weimar. They met to discuss how best to run Germany. This was the start of the **Weimar Republic**.

Information box 1: Communists

Communists believe in **Communism**. This is a political idea about how best to run a country.

- In a Communist country, everyone is equal (men <u>and</u> women) and everything is shared.
- There are no different classes and no great differences in wealth. As you might expect, this attracts poorer workers – Communist life sounds better than the one they've got!
- There is no private property and the government (or council) runs farms, factories and businesses for the benefit of all people.
- There is little need for money or laws because everyone lives a simple life, sharing all they have with others. Eventually, Communists believe that there will be no need for any governments or councils at all because people would live in harmony, only taking what they need and working as hard as they can.
- A belief in Communism or similar is sometimes known as **left wing**. For example, the **Spartacus League** was a left-wing political party.

Red is the traditional colour of Communism and Russia became the world's first Communist country in 1917 ... with their famous red flag.

Information box 2: Free Corps

The Free Corps was a group of bloodthirsty ex-soldiers who had recently come home from the Great War. They hated the Spartacus League (and Communists in general) because they blamed them for stirring up trouble in Germany towards the end of the war. The Free Corps argued that this trouble was a major reason for Germany's defeat. There were other Communist uprisings in Germany (in Bavaria in May 1919 and a 'red rising' in the Ruhr in March 1920), which the Free Corps ended with savage brutality.

▼ **Source B** *The Free Corps in action, 1919.*

FACT *Names, names, names*

Historians like to give names to different periods of time in a country's history, for example, Tudor England, Victorian Britain or Nazi Germany. Between 1919 and 1933, Germany was known as the Weimar Republic or Weimar Germany. *Weimar* was the town where the newly elected politicians first met after the end of the Great War. A *republic* is a country run by a parliament with no king, queen, kaiser or emperor.

WISE UP WORDS

- Free Corps Communists Spartacus League
  Weimar Republic democratic republic
  dictator Communism left wing

WORK

1 a Test your understanding of this double page by explaining the following terms:
   - Spartacus League
   - Free Corps

 b In your own words, explain why these two groups fought against each other.

2 a Why do you think Friedrich Ebert won the February 1919 election to become Germany's first president?

 b How did the 'Weimar Republic' get its name?

So how was the Weimar Republic governed?

In 1919, Germany's politicians drew up a set of rules for how Germany would be governed. This was called the Weimar **Constitution**. As you can see from the box below, it was a very different system from the way Germany used to be run when the Kaiser controlled everything. In fact, the Weimar Republic was one of the most democratic countries anywhere in the world.

The structure of the Weimar Constitution

The new Constitution was incredibly fair. All Germans had equal rights, including the right to vote. The fact that all women over the age of 20 could vote shows that Germany was more forward-thinking than many other countries. In Britain, for example, only women over the age of 28 could vote! However, the new system of government had several weaknesses.

The President (Head of State)
- elected every seven years
- controlled army, navy and air force
- stayed out of day-to-day running of the country. In a crisis, he could rule on his own – without getting the support of the Reichstag – using special 'emergency powers' known as **Article 48**

The Chancellor (Prime Minister)
- chosen by the President (usually from the political party with most votes at an election)
- responsible for day-to-day running of the country – law and order, taxation, schooling, health care and so on
- must have the support of at least half the politicians in the Reichstag to introduce new laws

The Reichstag
- introduced laws
- members of the Reichstag (MPs/politicians) were elected every four years
- the voting system used was called **Proportional Representation** (**PR**). This meant that the number of politicians each political party had in the Reichstag was based on the number of votes they had. For example, if a party won 10% of the votes, it was given 10% of the seats

The German people (the electorate)
- all men and women over the age of 20 could vote
- they elected the President and the politicians in the Reichstag
- the Constitution guaranteed them basic freedoms, such as free speech

---

Proportional Representation meant that lots of different political parties were able to win seats in the Reichstag. Sometimes there were over 20 different political parties all arguing over a single issue! This made it difficult to make decisions and introduce laws. In fact, between 1919 and 1933, no political party ever won more than half the votes in any election – and as a result, they didn't get more than half the seats. With no **majority**, the leading party had to do deals with smaller groups in order to get anything done. Again, this made decision-making a very slow process.

Also, many groups didn't like this new system of democracy, elections and parliament at all. In fact, they didn't like any sort of change. Some of the older army generals, judges, upper-class families, rich owners of big factories and university professors longed for the 'good old days' when the Kaiser ruled Germany. The new system of government was linked to the surrender at the end of the Great War. They wanted one strong leader like they had before the war (see **Source C**).

▼ **Source C** *From the BBC series* History File: Nazi Germany, *Episode One.*

"Politicians! What is this democracy? We never used to have democracy. We had strong leaders like the Kaiser. We never voted for him and was Germany ever so weak under the Kaiser? I spit on freedom — it's the patriotic thing to do!"

▼ **Source D** *A selection of political parties in Germany in the early 1920s. Their names are written in English but they have been given their German initials. Like political parties in Britain today, their beliefs and policies differed but the Social Democrats, the Democratic Party and the Centre Party tended to attract most votes in elections during the early and mid-1920s.*

LEFT WING							RIGHT WING
POLITICAL PARTY	COMMUNIST PARTY (KPD)	SOCIAL DEMOCRATIC PARTY (SPD)	GERMAN DEMOCRATIC PARTY (DDP)	CENTRE PARTY (ZENTRUM)	PEOPLE'S PARTY (DVP)	NATIONAL PEOPLE'S PARTY (DNVP)	NATIONAL SOCIALIST GERMAN WORKERS' PARTY (NSDAP OR NAZIS)
SUPPORTERS	Working class	Mostly working class	Middle class, for example, lawyers, writers and so on.	Catholics from all classes (Germany was largely a Catholic country).	Middle class, mainly businessmen	Middle and upper classes, some ex-soldiers	Unemployed, mainly ex-soldiers. Some support from middle and upper classes who feared the Communists.
ATTITUDE TO WEIMAR REPUBLIC Anti = against Pro = for	Anti-republic	Pro-republic Ebert, Weimar Germany's first President, was a Social Democrat.	Pro-republic	Pro-republic	Pro-republic, but would like a return to having a kaiser at some time in the future.	Anti-republic	Anti-republic
POLICIES	Thought Germany should be a Communist country and run by workers' councils, not by parliament.	Believed everyone was equal. Wanted democracy and reforms to help ordinary working-class Germans.	Believed in individual freedom – rights to hold peaceful meetings, form societies, freedom of speech and so on.	Supported the interests and beliefs of the Catholic Church.	Supporters of any policies that promoted trade and industry (and made them some money).	Wanted strong government, perhaps led by one strong politician or a kaiser again.	Wanted Germany to be a great nation again. Hated democracy and wanted strong government led by one man. Hated Communism because it states that all people are equal. Nazis believed that some races and nations were better than others. Wanted Germany to be a great military power once more.

WORK

1 **a** Explain what is meant by the terms:
Weimar Constitution • Proportional Representation
   b What is your opinion of Germany's new Weimar Constitution? **TOP TIP:** Don't just write 'It looks OK'! Try to have an opinion. Is it fair or unfair? Who benefits? What are its strengths and weaknesses? It is important in history to have your own opinion, after all, how often do you get asked in other lessons about your views? Remember, a good history student will always back up their opinions with evidence!

2 Look at **Source D**.
   a Which three major political parties did not support the new, democratic way Germany was governed?
   b Why did each of these parties dislike the Weimar Republic?

CLASSIC EXAM QUESTION

Describe the problems the Weimar Republic faced in the early 1920s.

WISE UP WORDS

• majority Proportional Representation Constitution Article 48

'Diktat'

Topic Focus

▶ This double page will help you to understand the ways in which the Treaty of Versailles affected Germany.

Exam Focus

▶ You should be able to explain why ordinary Germans disliked the Treaty of Versailles.

On 7 March 1919, France, Great Britain and America – the main winning countries of the Great War – announced what was going to happen to Germany – a losing country – for their part in the fighting.

Germany was to lose about 10% of its land, 12.5% of its population, 16% of its coal mines and nearly 50% of its iron industry. They were to lose all overseas colonies and most of their armed forces. They were even going to be forced to accept the blame for starting the war and pay for all the damage done in the fighting. The Germans were horrified … they didn't expect their punishment to be this tough!

So what could the German politicians do about the punishment? Did they *have* to accept it or was there an alternative? And how did ordinary people react to the news?

▼ **Source A** *The main points of the* **Treaty of Versailles**.
All other losing countries – Austria, Hungary, Turkey and Bulgaria – lost land, had their armed forces reduced and had to pay for war damage too. Only Germany took the blame for starting the war.

Land was to be taken away from Germany and given to her neighbours. This resulted in the country being cut in two (see map). Germany was also forbidden from joining with Austria again and all of Germany's overseas colonies were taken away.

Germany must accept blame for starting the war and pay **reparations** for the damage. A special group would meet to decide how much Germany must pay for their 'war guilt'.

Germany was to be banned from having an air force, tanks or submarines. They could only have a navy of six battleships and a tiny army of 100 000 men. German soldiers were not allowed into the Rhineland, a **demilitarised zone** near France.

The new German government was not invited to the peace discussions, which took place in the Palace of Versailles near Paris, France. Instead, they were told they had to accept their punishment or face invasion from Britain, France and the USA. Although many Germans would have preferred to fight again rather than accept such a harsh punishment, the new German government decided to sign the peace treaty – known as the Treaty of Versailles – rather than put the country through another war. With only an hour to go before the deadline for signing the treaty ran out, the German government sent a message to Paris saying they agreed to sign. Two German politicians travelled to France and signed the treaty on 28 June 1919.

As you can see, the Treaty of Versailles was designed to cripple Germany by taking away land, money and weapons. The winning countries, especially France and Britain, had worked hard to make sure that Germany would never be a threat to them again. The American President, who didn't want to punish Germany so severely, worried that Germany may seek revenge in the future. He was right to worry (see **Source B**)!

▼ **Source B** *From the front page of one of Germany's leading newspapers on the day the Treaty of Versailles was signed. The Hall of Mirrors is a huge mirrored room inside the Palace of Versailles.*

VENGEANCE GERMAN NATION!

Today, in the Hall of Mirrors, the disgraceful treaty is being signed. Do not forget it. The German people will regain their place amongst the nations, to which they are entitled. Then will come vengeance [revenge] for the shame of 1919.

Ordinary Germans hated the treaty and the people responsible for it. They called it a **diktat** – a dictated peace – because the Germans were ordered to sign the treaty without having a chance to discuss it. Some Germans even hated the German government for signing it. They said it showed how weak they were and accused them of 'stabbing their own country in the back'.

TOP EXAM TIP

The Treaty of Versailles is an ideal subject for a 'mind map' when you are revising for this topic.

▼ **Source C** *Karl Nagerl, a schoolboy in 1919, remembers how he felt at the end of the Great War.*

"It was a relief when the war was over. Now we had to see what the consequences of defeat were … when the terms of the Treaty of Versailles were announced, the German people were shocked at everything that was expected of us and dismayed at the payments we would have to make. They were sure to lead the German nation to ruin."

WISE UP WORDS

- reparations Treaty of Versailles diktat Kapp Putsch demilitarised zone

WORK

1 **a** Which part of the Treaty of Versailles was likely to make the German people feel angry?

 b Which part would make them feel insecure?

2 **a** Imagine that you run a German newspaper in 1919 that does not support the German government. Design a front-page news story reporting on the Treaty of Versailles. It should include:

- a powerful headline that captures the mood of ordinary Germans;
- a strong opening paragraph that sums up the treaty (see **Source B**);
- a summary of the main points of the treaty;
- an explanation of why so many Germans are shocked, angry and humiliated. You might even include a few interviews here;
- a comment on the current leaders of Germany – why not draw your own political cartoon?

 b If you ran a German newspaper that *supported* the German government, in what ways would your news story be different?

1923: The Weimar Republic in trouble

Topic Focus

▸ These pages will help you to understand the problems that 'hyperinflation' caused Germany.

Exam Focus

▸ You must be able to explain the link between the French invasion of the Ruhr and Germany's problems with 'hyperinflation'.

In December 1921, a loaf of bread in Berlin would cost about four marks. This was an acceptable price for an ordinary food item that most Germans would eat on a regular basis. By September 1923, a loaf of bread cost about 1 500 000 marks. That's right ... one and a half *million* marks! Unbelievably, by November 1923, a loaf cost 201 000 000 000 marks!

So what caused a loaf of bread – and everything else that Germans could buy – to shoot up in price so much? How did **hyperinflation**, as these price rises were known, affect different groups in German society? And how did ordinary Germans feel about their government during this period?

In the peace treaty at the end of the Great War, Germany was ordered to pay for all the damage done by the fighting. In 1921, it was announced that they had to pay 132 billion gold marks – or £6 600 000 000 – in equal yearly instalments for the next 66 years! Later that year, the German government scraped together their first instalment of two billion gold marks and handed it over to France and Belgium. These were the two countries that had been most damaged by the fighting. Some of it was gold but most of it was in goods like coal, iron and wood.

In January 1923, Germany announced that they couldn't afford to pay any more. The French and Belgians didn't believe them and vowed to force Germany to pay. A few days later, 60 000 French and Belgian soldiers marched into the Ruhr, a rich, industrial area of Germany, full of coal mines and factories. They had decided to take what was owed to them by force. The consequences of this invasion were remarkable. They led to the amazing hyperinflation of 1923 and a 200 billion-mark loaf of bread! To understand how this happened, study the cartoons very carefully.

1

French and Belgian soldiers began to take what was owed to them from Germany back to France.

2

The German government ordered its workers in the Ruhr to go on strike and not help the soldiers remove goods from the country. This was called **passive resistance**.

to all German workers in the Ruhr
GO ON STRIKE
Signed German government.

3

Krupp Steelworks

French and Belgian soldiers were tough with the strikers. Over 100 of them were killed and 150 000 people were thrown out of their homes as a punishment.

4

The German government met to discuss the crisis. They promised to continue paying the workers on strike. To make matters worse, the government was running short of money because the Ruhr wasn't producing coal, iron and steel to sell to other nations.

Reichstag

We must help workers in the Ruhr.

They are on strike and earning no money because we asked them to.

5

To pay their striking workers, the government printed large amounts of money – but this caused lots of problems.

6

The striking workers began to spend their money – quickly. They were being paid for not working and wanted to spend, spend, spend! In response, shopkeepers began to put up their prices.

I'll spend it while there are still goods in the shops.

If they've got all this money to spend, I'll raise my prices.

LOAF.
150 marks
250 marks
770 marks
2,150 marks
4,200 marks

7

Prices are rising.

We must print more money to help people buy things.

As shops raised their prices all over Germany, the government responded by printing even more money. The more money the government printed, the faster prices went up.

8

The faster prices went up, the faster people spent their wages. Soon workers were being paid twice a day. They carried their wages around in wheelbarrows. The price of goods could rise between joining the back of a queue and reaching the front!

This isn't even enough to buy me a decent meal.

Café

Menu

9

I've worked hard all my life and saved money in the bank – now it won't buy me anything because prices are so high.

As you might expect, the German government and the Weimar politicians lost a lot of support in 1923 as people looked for someone to blame.

WORK

Rearrange the following statements in the correct order to reveal a basic summary of the cause of hyperinflation in Germany in 1923.

- Soon prices were inflating so fast that it became known as *hyper*inflation.
- As workers spent money in shops, shopkeepers put up prices.
- German workers were ordered to go on strike in the Ruhr but continued to get paid.
- French and Belgian troops invaded the Ruhr in response to the German government's failure to pay the reparations they owed.
- The German government printed lots of money to pay striking workers AND pay the money they owed France and Belgium.
- The German government printed even more money ... so shops raised their prices again.

German money was worthless by November 1923. The government had printed so much that it lost all its value. People started to use it to light their fire or make paper aeroplanes or kites to fly (see **Source A**). Not surprisingly, many Germans blamed their government for the mess because it was their decision to call a strike in the Ruhr and then to print so much money. For most, 1923 was the worst year since the end of the Great War and their democratically elected politicians seemed to have caused their problems.

▼ **Source A** *A woman using worthless German banknotes to light her fire in 1923.*

▶ **Source B** *A German banknote issued in 1923. Can you see how much it is worth?*

▼ **Source C** *The memories of a German writer in 1923.*

"Two women were carrying a laundry basket filled to the top with banknotes. Seeing a crowd standing round a shop window, they put down the basket for a moment to see if there was anything they could buy. When they turned around a few moments later, they found the money was untouched, but the basket had been stolen."

▼ **Source D** *Price for a loaf of bread and one egg in Germany, 1918–1923.*

1918 – 0.6 marks
1921 – 4 marks
1922 – 163 marks
January 1923 – 250 marks
July 1923 – 3456 marks
September 1923 – 1 512 000 marks
November 1923 – 201 000 000 000 marks

1914 – 0.9 marks
1921 – 1.6 marks
1922 – 7 marks
July 1923 – 5000 marks
September 1923 – 4 000 000 marks
November 1923 – 320 000 000 000 marks

How did hyperinflation affect different people?

LOSERS	WINNERS
People with savings in the bank were the biggest losers. Some people had saved all their lives to get 1000 marks in the bank – by 1923, it wouldn't even buy them a loaf of bread. Elderly people who lived on fixed pensions found their income wouldn't buy them what they needed any more. Many small businesses collapsed as normal trade became impossible because of the daily price changes.	People who had borrowed money found it very easy to pay off their debts. If a person had borrowed 10 000 marks in 1920 (a lot of money then), they could now pay off their debt with one banknote!

▲ **Source E** *Hyperinflation affected different people in different ways. However, there were far more losers than winners.*

▼ **Source F** *A modern historian writing about the hyperinflation crisis of 1923.*

"Millions of people faced starvation as a result of the hyperinflation. People such as pensioners who were living on fixed incomes found that prices rose much faster than their earnings. So even if they could afford to buy food, they might not be able to pay for the gas to cook it. They lived in unheated houses because they couldn't afford coal and they froze because they couldn't afford to buy clothes. The well-to-do [richer] suffered along with the poor. People with thousands in the bank in 1918 now found their savings would not even buy a slice of bread or a piece of coal."

TOP EXAM TIP

The situation in Germany in 1923 is a good example of how different factors can sometimes link together. The reparations laid down by the Treaty of Versailles linked to the invasion of the Ruhr ... which linked to the hyperinflation crisis.

It was at this very moment – November 1923 – that a 34-year-old ex-soldier would try to overthrow the German government and take control of the country. He felt he could do a much better job. His name was Adolf Hitler and he was the leader of a political group nicknamed the Nazis.

WISE UP WORDS

• hyperinflation   passive resistance

WORK

1 Look at **Source A**.
   a What is the woman in the photograph doing?
   b Why has she chosen to do this, rather than spend her money in the shops?

2 Look at **Source B**. The German banknote on the right was issued at the end of August 1923. It was worth 10 000 000 marks.
   a Using **Source D** to help you, work out how many eggs you could have bought with this banknote in September 1923.
   b How many eggs could you have bought in November 1923?

3 Explain how the following people would have been affected by hyperinflation:
   i) an elderly woman, living alone on her fixed pension; ii) a school leaver who was looking for their first job; iii) a farmer who had borrowed money in 1919 and owed 5000 marks; iv) a married couple who had saved all their lives for retirement and had 20 000 marks in the bank.

4 Why do you think hyperinflation turned many ordinary Germans against their government?

Who was Adolf Hitler?

Topic Focus

▸ To gain an understanding of Hitler's life and family.

Exam Focus

▸ To be able to describe Hitler's early life, and the effect it had on him as an adult.

Adolf Hitler is one of the most **infamous** men in history. His leadership of Germany and his role in the outbreak of World War Two are the most widely studied parts of twentieth-century history. But to fully understand his rise to power, you must understand his background.

So what was his family like? What were his ambitions as a young man? How close did he come to fulfilling these ambitions? And how did he first get involved in politics?

Adolf Hitler was born on 20 April 1889 in Braunau, a small town in Austria, near to the German border. He went to an ordinary school and enjoyed ordinary things – reading, listening to music, painting and boxing. His favourite two subjects at school were Art and History. His father was a hard-drinking bully who beat his son. He died when Hitler was 14. Hitler's mother spoiled him and was determined he should get good grades at school and a well-paid job. However, he failed his examinations and left school at 16. His mother died when he was 17. After her death, Hitler left his hometown and travelled to Vienna, the capital city of Austria, to look for work. He had dreams of becoming a famous painter.

▸ **Source A** *Hitler, circled, at school in 1899 aged ten. He was in the local church choir for five years.*

▾ **Source B** *Comments from one of Hitler's teachers.*

> "He always wanted his own way. He was boastful, bad-tempered and lazy … he ignored advice and got angry if he was told off. At the same time, he demanded complete obedience from his fellow pupils."

▼ **_Source C_** *Hitler, remembering his schoolteachers in an interview in 1941. He hated all of his teachers, except his History teacher.*

> "My teachers did not understand young people – their one aim was to stuff our brains and turn us into educated apes – like themselves."

▼ **_Source D_** *Hitler's father, Alois, worked as a postman and for Austrian customs. He was illegitimate (his parents weren't married) and Alois took his mother's surname of Schicklgruber. He later changed it to Hitler. Adolf was always grateful to his father for this. He said it was easy to remember!*

Hitler arrived in Vienna in 1907 and tried to pass the entrance exams for the Vienna Art Academy, one of Europe's best art colleges. He failed twice. Short of money, he ended up living in a hostel for tramps.

For the next few years, he earned money any way he could – he painted postcards to sell in the streets, cleaned windows and swept up snow in the winter or leaves in the autumn. He soon became jealous and full of hatred. He hated people of foreign races and different religions, especially Jews. He felt they were ruining Austria by taking all the jobs and introducing their way of life. He was jealous of foreigners who were making something better of their lives than he was!

▼ **_Source E_** *One of Hitler's paintings. He was a good artist – but not good enough to win a place at the Vienna Art Academy.*

▼ **Source F** *Letter from Hitler to a friend in July, 1908.*

"Dear Friend,

To begin with, I am still in Vienna and am staying on. Still, I am enjoying my life ... I have no other news to tell you except that I caught a gang of bedbugs floating dead in my own blood and that my teeth are chattering."

Hitler left Austria in 1913 to avoid compulsory service in the Austrian army. He went to live in Munich in Germany. When the Great War started in 1914, he decided to be a soldier after all and volunteered to join the German army.

Hitler worked all through the war, doing the dangerous job of taking messages between the trenches. He was wounded several times, once when a piece of metal sliced through his cheek nearly killing him. In total, he won six medals, including two Iron Crosses, the highest bravery award in the German army.

▼ **Source G** *A photograph of Hitler (right) and some army pals in 1914.*

TOP EXAM TIP

It is always very useful to learn about a person's background ... it can often give you a valuable insight into the development of their character and actions in later life.

▼ **Source H** *A report on Hitler by his Commanding Officer during the Great War.*

"**Report on Lance Corporal Hitler, Third Company (Volunteers), 1916**

Hitler has been with the regiment since 1914 and has fought splendidly in all the battles in which he has taken part.

As a messenger, he was always ready to carry messages in the most difficult positions at great risk to his own life.

He received the Iron Cross (2nd Class) on 2 December 1914 and I now feel he is worthy of receiving the Iron Cross (1st Class)."

▼ **Source I** *Hitler was in hospital when the war ended in November 1918, temporarily blinded in a gas attack. He heard the news from a visitor. Many were delighted that the war was over. Others, like Hitler, were appalled because they thought the Germans could still win. Hitler blamed Germany's defeat on weak German politicians … and of course, the Jews!*

"What? Was such a thing possible? I broke down completely … darkness surrounded me as I staggered and stumbled back to my ward and buried my head between the blankets and the pillow. I had not cried since the day I stood beside my mother's grave."

Hitler stayed in the army after the war. This was a time when many new political groups and parties were being created all over Germany. The government was worried about some of them in case they were violent or tried to start a revolution. Based in Munich, Hitler worked as a V-man – an army spy whose job was to investigate these new political groups. One group he investigated in May 1919 wasn't dangerous at all – they only had a few members and funds of only 7.5 marks – about £4. They were called the German Workers' Party.

WISE UP WORD
- infamous

WORK

1 Here is a list of interesting dates in Adolf Hitler's life up to 1919.

1914 • 1889 • 1918 • 1907 • 1906 • 1899 • 1903 • 1919 • 1913 • 1905

Write each date on a separate line in the correct chronological order. Beside each date, write what happened in that year.

2 Look below at the three interpretations of Hitler's life up to 1919.
   i) 'Hitler was a vicious racist who was filled with hatred from an early age.'
   ii) 'Hitler had a good family background and had led a perfectly normal life up to 1919.'
   iii) 'Hitler was a brave man who had had a tough life up to 1919.'
   a Which opinion do you MOST agree with? Give reasons for your answer.
   b Which opinion do you LEAST agree with? Again, give reasons for your answer.

3 Choose two events in Hitler's life so far that you would regard as important turning points. Explain why each event you have chosen was so important.

The Nazi Party

Topic Focus

▶ To understand three main beliefs of the Nazis.

Exam Focus

▶ Can you explain how Hitler chaned the Nazi party in the early 1920s?
Why did the Munich Putsch fail?

In May 1919, Hitler was sent on a spying mission by the German army. His job was to investigate whether a new political party – the German Workers' Party – was dangerous or not. He soon discovered that they were no threat to the government at all. They only had a few members, hardly any money, no party programme or philosophy, no leaflets, no posters – not even a symbol or flag. But within two years, Hitler had taken over the German Workers' Party and transformed it. Within four years, he and fellow party members would try to take over Germany. How was this possible?

Hitler enters politics

The German Workers' Party that Hitler first visited in May 1919 had only been started a few months before by a railway worker called Anton Drexler. It was one of many small political parties in and around Munich at this time. The small group met in beer halls and Hitler attended regularly because he liked what was being said. People made speeches about how the Treaty of Versailles made Germany weak and how the country would become a great nation once more. This appealed to Hitler, a wounded and defeated ex-soldier who hated the politicians who agreed to end a war he loved … and then signed the terrible Treaty of Versailles, which made Germany weak and defenceless.

Hitler soon joined the party, becoming their 55th member (see **Source A**) and threw himself into the task of building up the membership. He put advertisements in newspapers, stuck posters on walls and held public meetings all over Munich. Hitler was a brilliant speaker who could fascinate his audience with powerful and interesting speeches. In the early days of radio, and with no television, this was a very important skill. He even persuaded the party to buy a newspaper – the *Munich Observer* – to put forward their views. Before long, Hitler was running the party. He then made more key changes.

▶ **Source A** *Hitler's membership card for the German Workers' Party (Deutsche Arbeiter Partei or DAP). Hitler always claimed he was the seventh member, but his card shows that he was member number 555. However, most historians agree that the party started numbering at 500 to make it look like they had more members.*

The Nazis are born

Firstly, the party's name was extended to the Nationalsozialistische Deutsche Arbeiter Partei or National Socialist German Workers' Party and a party programme was issued (see **Source D**). "Nazi Party" is in fact a nickname – a shortened version of the full name. Secondly, a specially designed flag and symbol – the **swastika** – was unveiled in order to attract attention (see **Source E**). Finally, Hitler set up a private army of thugs to beat up anyone who disagreed with him. They were known as the **Sturm Abteilung** (**SA**) or Storm Troopers and wore a brown uniform with swastika armbands. This violent bunch of mostly ex-soldiers would guard Hitler's meetings against people from other political parties who came to boo and shout abuse at him.

Under Hitler's influence, the Nazi Party (as it became known) grew and grew. There were 3000 members in 1920 and 5000 in 1921. Although based in Munich, there were soon members all over Germany. By 1923, Hitler felt confident enough in his own support – and his own abilities – to try to take over Munich … and then Germany!

▼ **Source B** *A comment made by Anton Drexler when he first heard Hitler speak.*

> "My God! He's got a big gob. We could make good use of him!"

▼ **Source C** *A man comments on how he felt when listening to Hitler speak in 1922.*

> "He was holding us under a hypnotic spell. I forgot everything but the man; then, glancing around, I saw that his magnetism was holding these thousands as one."

▼ **Source D** *Extracts from the Twenty-Five Point Programme of the Nazi Party. This was a political manifesto, a list of beliefs, ideas and promises. Hitler wasn't interested in all of them, but saw them as a way of attracting more support.*

TWENTY-FIVE POINT PROGRAMME (MAIN POINTS)

- ALL GERMANS SHOULD BE UNITED IN ONE COUNTRY.
- THE TREATY OF VERSAILLES SHOULD BE DESTROYED.
- WE NEED MORE LAND FOR OUR GROWING POPULATION TO LIVE ON.
- ONLY THOSE OF GERMAN BLOOD CAN BELONG TO THE GERMAN NATION; NO JEWS CAN BELONG.
- NON-GERMANS CANNOT BE ALLOWED TO LIVE IN GERMANY.
- THE GOVERNMENT MUST PROVIDE JOBS FOR EVERYONE AND EVERYONE MUST WORK.
- NO ONE SHOULD RECEIVE MONEY WITHOUT WORKING.
- NO ONE IS ALLOWED TO MAKE MONEY OUT OF WAR.
- ALL BIG BUSINESSES SHOULD BE RUN BY THE GOVERNMENT AND ANY PROFITS SHARED OUT AMONGST THE WORKERS.
- THERE SHOULD BE HIGHER OLD AGE PENSIONS.
- THE GOVERNMENT SHOULD LOOK AFTER MOTHERS AND CHILDREN.
- THERE SHOULD BE A LARGE ARMY.
- THERE SHOULD BE A STRONG, TOUGH CENTRAL GOVERNMENT FOR GERMANY LED BY ONE MAN.
- COMMUNISM MUST BE DESTROYED. THEIR BELIEF IN EQUALITY IS WRONG — SOME RACES AND NATIONS ARE BETTER THAN OTHERS AND DESERVE TO CONQUER THEM.

▼ **Source E** *The famous swastika or crooked cross flag. The swastika is, in fact, an ancient religious symbol meaning 'well-being'. Hitler wanted something eye-catching and simple to draw.*

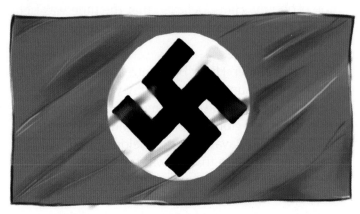

WISE UP WORDS

- swastika   Sturm Abteilung

WORK

1   Look at **Source A.** Why do you think Hitler always claimed he was the seventh member of the German Workers' Party when his membership card said he was member number 555?

2   **a**   Why do you think Hitler decided to join the German Workers' Party?

   b   What changes did Hitler make to the German Workers' Party? For each change, explain *why* you think each change was made.

3   Look at **Source D.**

   a   Choose five of the ideas on the Twenty-Five Point Programme of the Nazi Party. For each of your chosen points, write who it would appeal to and why. For example, the creation of a large army would appeal to many ex-soldiers or ordinary Germans who felt humiliated that Germany was banned from having a large army according to the Treaty of Versailles.

   b   Why would Hitler include some ideas in the Programme even if he didn't believe in them?

In November 1923, Hitler felt the Nazis were strong enough to take over Germany. This was a time when Germany was in chaos – the French had invaded the Ruhr and hyperinflation was crippling the economy. Hitler believed that the time was right to get rid of such a poor government and replace it with the Nazis.

On 8 November, Hitler burst into a meeting in a beer hall in Munich where Gustav von Kahr, the head of the Bavarian government, was speaking (Bavaria is a region of Germany; Munich is the biggest city in Bavaria). Hitler held a gun to Kahr's head and told him that he was taking over Bavaria. He then said he would march to Berlin and take over the whole country (Berlin was – and is – the capital of the whole of Germany). Kahr didn't say anything so Hitler locked him in a cupboard! Then General Ludendorff, a great German war hero who knew about the plan, walked in and said he supported Hitler. Around Munich, Hitler's Storm Troopers took control of government buildings and arrested officials (see **Source G**).

The next morning, things started to go wrong. Kahr escaped during the night and called in the troops. When Hitler and about 2000 supporters began their march through Munich's streets, they were met by armed police. After a short gun battle, three policemen and 16 Nazis lay dead, Hitler was wounded (with a dislocated shoulder) and he and Ludendorff were arrested and taken to prison. The Munich **Putsch**, as it became known, was over … and Hitler was about to go on trial for treason.

▼ **Source F** *Part of a speech Hitler gave on the night of 8 November 1923. Who do you think are the November Criminals?*

> "Now I am going to carry out the promise I made five years ago when I was a blind cripple in the army hospital: to neither rest nor sleep until the November Criminals have been hurled to the ground, until on the ruins of the pitiful Germany of today has risen a Germany of power and greatness."

▼ **Source G** *Nazi Storm Troopers (note their swastika armbands) arrest the Mayor of Munich (in the dark coat) on 9 November 1923.*

Hitler's trial lasted 24 days. It was a media sensation, reported in newspapers all over Germany. This was the largest audience Hitler had ever had – and he intended to take full advantage of it! He used every opportunity to criticise the government and put across his political views. His tactics seemed to work and he impressed the judges. Ludendorff was set free and Hitler was sent to prison for just five years (he could have been executed for such a serious crime). Other Nazis got away with equally light sentences.

FACT *Who voted 'Nazi'?*

You must remember that the Nazis were a genuine political party that people could vote for – not just a group of men who tried to take over Germany. In the early days, the Nazis appealed to ex-soldiers who wanted a strong leadership and a new, improved army. They appealed to women who were flattered by his pledge to make the family more important and racists who supported Hitler's views on Jews. He also tried to attract votes from farmers and businessmen by promising to use his Storm Troopers to protect their land and property at all costs. He didn't seem to get too much support though – in May 1924, there were 32 Nazi politicians in parliament, dropping to 14 by 1925. By 1928, there were only 12 with the Nazis, who were only getting 2% of the votes!

▼ **Source H** *The sort of things Hitler said at his trial. Who was Hitler referring to as the 'traitors of 1918'?*

> "There is no such thing as treason against the traitors of 1918 … I feel myself the best of Germans who wants the best for the German people … History will tear to tatters the verdict of this court!"

Hitler spent some of his time in Landsberg prison sorting out his ideas, reading books and seeing as many visitors as he wished. He also wrote a book called **Mein Kampf** (*My Struggle*), which describes his life story and his political views (see **Source I**). He was released from prison in December 1924 after serving just nine months. The failure of his Munich Putsch and his time in prison taught Hitler a valuable lesson. He realised he had to change his strategy. The Nazis would have to stand in elections and win votes, just like any other political party. They would have to win power democratically, instead of grabbing it by force.

▼ **Source I** *The main views contained in* Mein Kampf. *It is a poorly written book that also contains his opinions on, among other things, boxing and sexually transmitted diseases. You can still purchase a copy today!*

All Germans all over the world must be united under one leader.

The Treaty of Versailles is unfair and too harsh. It must be ignored.

All Jews and Communists must be destroyed, as they are the cause of many of Germany's problems, including their loss in the Great War.

The Germans are a master race of super-humans called **Aryans.** They must have whatever land they need to breed and expand.

▼ **Source J** *Hitler speaking in 1925.*

> "Instead of working to achieve power by armed rebellion, we shall have to hold our noses and enter the Reichstag [parliament] … outvoting them may take longer than outshooting them but sooner or later we shall have a majority, and after that — Germany."

WISE UP WORDS

- Mein Kampf   Putsch   Aryans

WORK

1 It is 1923. Choose to be either a supporter or an opponent of Hitler and the Nazis. Write to a friend in Britain explaining:
   - who Hitler and the Nazis are;
   - what they stand for;
   - who supports them and why;
   - what they were trying to do in Munich in November 1923;
   - about Hitler's trial and punishment.

   Obviously, the opinions expressed by a supporter of Hitler will differ from those given by someone who hated him. When you have completed this task, compare your letter with someone who had a different opinion of Hitler, the Nazis and the Munich Putsch.

2 **a** What is *Mein Kampf*?
   b Why do you think Hitler chose this title?
   c Draw your own diagram, similar to the one in **Source I**, which summarises the main ideas expressed by Hitler in *Mein Kampf*. You must *not* use more than 30 words!

3 Look at **Source J**. What can you learn from this source about Hitler's methods of trying to achieve power after the Munich Putsch?

4 Describe the Munich (Beer Hall) Putsch, 1923.

Germany recovers

Topic Focus

▸ To understand the reasons why Germany was more economically stable from 1924 to 1929.

Exam Focus

▸ To be able to explain the potential threats to Germany's recovery, and also to understand Gustav Stresemann's solutions which helped aid recovery.

1923 was a bad year in Germany. The French had invaded the Ruhr, one of Germany's richest industrial areas; hyperinflation had made money worthless and different political groups continued to cause trouble and think they could do a better job than the government. The Nazis had even tried to start a revolution and take over the country! But things didn't get any worse in Germany. In fact, after 1923, things started to get a lot better. Most historians put Germany's recovery down to the influence and hard work of one man – Gustav Stresemann. So how did he do it?

◀ **_Source A_** _Gustav Stresemann. In 1923, he became Germany's Chancellor. Later he was Foreign Minister from 1924 to 1929. He was awarded the Nobel Peace Prize in 1926._

Problem 1: Hyperinflation

Stresemann's solution: he stopped the printing of paper money and replaced all old money with a new currency called the Rentenmark. One Rentenmark replaced 1000 billion marks.

Success? Yes, Germans quickly accepted their new currency and hyperinflation ended. However, people who had lost all their savings never got their money back ... and forever blamed Stresemann and his government!

Problem 2: The French troops in the Ruhr

Stresemann's solution: he knew that French troops had invaded the Ruhr because Germany had not kept up their reparation payments. In 1924, Stresemann attended a meeting with French, British and American leaders. The result was the **Dawes Plan**, which allowed the Germans to only pay what they could afford. They also had longer to pay.

Success? Yes, French troops left the Ruhr. However, some Germans thought Stresemann had 'given in' to the French by not demanding a complete end to all reparations – many thought Germany shouldn't be paying anything at all! In 1929, the **Young Plan** further reduced the amount Germany owed ... but they still had to pay up to 1988!

Problem 3: No one trusted the Germans

Stresemann's solution: he tried to improve Germany's relationship with other countries.

- In 1925, Germany signed the **Locarno Pact** with Britain, France, Belgium and Italy. They promised not to invade each other.

- In 1926, Germany was allowed to join the League of Nations, an international peacekeeping organisation.

- In 1928, Germany, along with 64 other countries, signed the **Kellogg-Briand Pact**. They all agreed not to go to war unless in self-defence.

Success? Germany definitely became a major European power again under Stresemann. The **League of Nations** even gave Germany 'great power status', which meant they took part in major decisions. However, some Germans criticised Stresemann for not demanding some of the land back from countries that had taken it from Germany at the end of the Great War!

> The League of Nations Welcomes **GERMANY**

Problem 4: German industry was in trouble after the Great War – factories were run down, there were few jobs and poor schools, housing and hospitals.

Stresemann's solution: He organised big loans from America (this was part of the Dawes Plan). The Germans built new factories, housing, hospitals, schools and roads. This meant more jobs with Germans earning more money. Even some American companies (like Ford and Gillette) set up factories in Germany.

Success? Slowly, Germany became more prosperous. Some called it a 'golden age'. A night out in Berlin in the late 1920s – cinemas, music halls, night clubs, beer halls, galleries – was meant to be one of the greatest experiences in the world! However, some – even Stresemann himself – feared that Germany relied on American loans too much. What if the Americans suddenly wanted their money back?

Stresemann, one of Germany's most able and hard-working politicians, died of a heart attack in 1929. His time as Chancellor and later foreign minister had seen Germany enter a new era of peace and prosperity. Indeed, there were no attempts to overthrow the government between 1924 and 1929. Hitler and his Nazis meanwhile had become a bit of a national joke after their failed attempt to take over Germany in 1923. Hitler found it difficult to persuade Germans they needed him as their saviour when the country was doing so well. In 1924, about 5% of Germans voted for the Nazis. By 1928, their support had dropped – only 2% of Germans were voting for them ... but their time would come!

▼ **_Source B_** *From a speech by Gustav Stresemann in 1928.*

> "Germany is dancing on a volcano. If America calls in their loans, a large section of our economy would collapse."

WISE UP WORDS

- Dawes Plan   Young Plan   Locarno Pact
  Kellogg-Briand Pact   League of Nations

WORK

1 Copy and complete the table below. On the last column, you must give Stresemann a star rating to show how successful you think he was.

2 Suggest why the Nazis only got 2% of the votes in the 1928 elections, even though they were a highly organised party with over 100 000 members.

Problem	Stresemann's policy	Was it a success, a failure or a bit of both? Explain fully.	Rating ***** = fantastic solution * = poor solution
1) Hyperinflation			
2) French occupation of the Ruhr			
3) Germany's poor relationship with other countries			
4) German industry short of investment			

3 To what extent did Stresemann succeed in solving the problems faced by the Weimar Republic?

Germany and the Great Depression

Topic Focus

▶ To remember how the Great Depression affected Germany.

Exam Focus

▶ You must be able to explain the link between the causes of the Great Depression, and how it helped Hitler and the Nazis.

From 1924 onwards, foreign banks lent huge amounts of money to Germany. Most of it was from America. The money meant that Germany could build factories and businesses and this created jobs. For many Germans then, the years immediately after 1924 turned out to be good ones with more jobs, more money and a better standard of living. However, in 1929, disaster struck. Within three years, over six million people would be out of work. So how did Germany go from 'boom' to 'bust'? What caused disaster to strike? And how did the Great Depression help Adolf Hitler?

America had grown rich after the Great War. Their factories sold goods such as cars, fridges, radios and wristwatches in America and all over the world. Some Americans even had money to spare and bought shares in companies and businesses hoping to make a profit. Some borrowed money from banks in order to join this 'share-buying craze'. In October 1929, things started to go wrong. Many Americans hadn't made as much as they'd hoped from their shares and decided to sell them … fast! But the more they sold, the more the share price dropped (try selling something that no one wants!). Millions of Americans couldn't sell their shares for as much as they'd paid for them. Some couldn't pay the banks back either and were left ruined as debt collectors took their cars and homes. Soon, many Americans couldn't afford to buy any new goods at all and as a result, firms went out of business and millions lost their jobs.

Americans couldn't afford to buy any foreign goods either … including those from Germany. Soon German factories had to close down and Germans lost their jobs. To make matters worse, American banks demanded back all the money it had lent to Germany. Thousands more German businesses collapsed because they had no money to keep them going. Soon, people were living on streets – cold, hungry … and angry!

This sudden slump in world trade was known as the Great Depression. America, Germany, Britain, Italy, Japan and many other countries were hit very hard. Unemployment shot up in all these countries as factory after factory closed when countries stopped trading with each other. In Britain, unemployment had shot up to over three million by 1932. In Germany, it had grown to six million! Not surprisingly, unemployment and hunger changed the way Germans thought and behaved. Once again, people blamed the government and the politicians for their problems. They started listening to political parties whose leaders promised them solutions to all Germany's problems. One of these men was Adolf Hitler. 'I'll provide you with work and bread' was Hitler's seductive promise, 'if you vote for me!'

▼ **_Source A_** _Unemployment in Germany, 1928–1932._

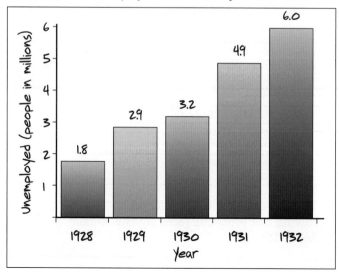

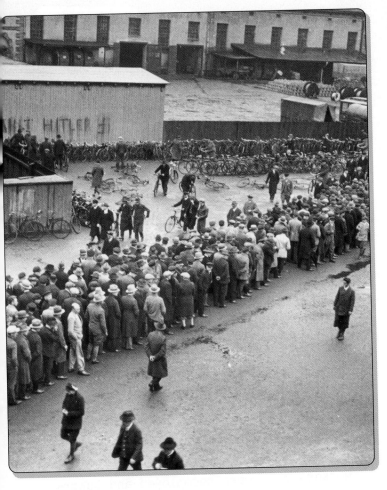

▲ **Source B** *Unemployed people in Hanover queue to get a bowl of soup and bread in 1932. Can you see what graffiti someone has painted on the warehouse wall?*

▼ **Source C** *Adapted from the British historian Alan Bullock.*

"… men standing hopelessly on the street corners of every industrial town in Germany; houses without food or warmth; boys and girls without any chance of a job … one may soon begin to guess the worry and bitterness burned into the minds of millions of ordinary German working men and women."

TOP EXAM TIP

The Great Depression is one of the key factors which helped Hitler into power. Ensure you know how it helped him.

FACT *Crash!*

The problems in October 1929 associated with buying and selling shares is often known as the Wall Street Crash. Wall Street is a famous road in New York where people go to buy and sell shares. A 'crash' is a term that Americans often use when things go wrong. We sometimes use the word 'crash' in the UK when our computer or mobile phone stops working properly!

▼ **Source D** *From the BBC series* History File: Nazi Germany, *Episode One.*

"Germany in the late 1920s — music, theatre, cinema and cabaret. But then, on 24 October 1929, Wall Street crashed! The worldwide depression that followed hit Germany hardest of all. With some satisfaction, Hitler realised his day had come. In three years, German production halved, unemployment rose to 6½ million. 17 million — a third of the population — were supported by dole money … in the face of depression, the German people looked for new solutions."

WORK

1. Explain in your own words why the German economy collapsed in 1929–1930. You could present your answer as an illustrated diagram, a flow chart or even a mini essay.

2. Look at **Source B**.

   a. Make up a conversation between two of the men in the queue in which they discuss:
      - how they lost their jobs;
      - what life is like for them during the Depression;
      - what they think about the man who is mentioned in the graffiti they can see on the warehouse wall!

      Don't be afraid to use your imagination. You might have to make up a few of the details but if you're sensible with this, you can have a good giggle comparing your conversations with others or even acting them out!

   b. How useful is **Source B** as evidence of unemployment in Germany in 1932?

3. Look at **Source D**. What do you think is meant by the phrase 'the German people looked for new solutions'?

Enter the Nazis

Topic Focus

▸ To look at the reasons Hitler became Chancellor of Germany in 1933.

Exam Focus

▸ What do you think was the most important factor in allowing Hitler to become Chancellor, and why?

In 1928, Hitler and the Nazis were very well known ... but they were still only the eighth most popular political party in Germany. They got only 800 000 votes in elections, with less than 3% of the population voting for them. In 1928, few Germans would have predicted that Hitler would become leader of Germany!

Yet, by July 1932, the Nazis were the most popular party, recording nearly 14 million votes. On 30 January 1933, Hitler was invited to be Chancellor, Germany's second highest political position, second only to the ageing President Hindenburg. How did this happen?

A number of different factors combined to help Hitler become Germany's Chancellor. Study them carefully. You will be asked to complete a summary task based on these factors.

FACTOR NO. 1 The Depression

The Depression hit Germany hard. Businesses collapsed, unemployment soared and banks closed. But this was just what Hitler wanted! Those voters who had ignored Hitler in the 1920s because they thought his ideas were too extreme now started listening to him ... and voting for him!

▾ **Source A** *From the BBC documentary series* The Nazis: A Warning from History.

▾ **Source B** *Comments of a student in 1972, on his experience in Germany in the 1930s.*

"What did he promise? Work and bread for the masses, for the millions of workers that were unemployed and hungry at that time. Nowadays, work and bread doesn't mean very much but at the time it was an absolute necessity — a basic need ... and this promise that wouldn't make any sense today — then it sounded like a promise of paradise."

"The Nazis were helped by circumstance ... Germany suffered [when] the Wall Street Crash started a worldwide economic slump [depression]. The Americans called in their loans, German unemployment rose to $5\frac{1}{2}$ million in 1931 ... and then, just when it seemed things couldn't get any worse, they did. The five major banks crashed in 1931. More than 20 000 German businesses folded. Now the middle class was suffering.... In the economic crisis, the Nazis' votes increased. They still said the same — Versailles was a crime, Jews should be persecuted, Germany must be reborn. Their message hadn't changed, it was just that now more Germans were ready to hear it."

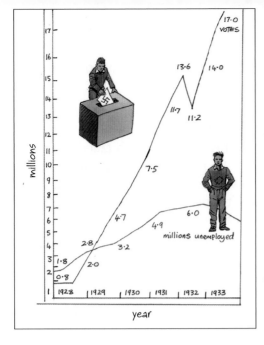

▲ **Source C** *The relationship between unemployment and votes for the Nazis.*

"It was collapse. People said, 'It can't go on like this'. Then the debate began about the need for a strong man. And the call for a strong man became louder and louder because democracy was achieving nothing."

▼ **Source F** *From the BBC documentary series* The Nazis: A Warning from History.

"It wasn't just the Nazis who began to do well. The Communists started to pick up votes too. Something sinister was happening to this new democracy – it seemed to be splitting apart as voters rushed to the extremes."

FACTOR NO. 2 Germans were unhappy with the government

The politicians couldn't seem to agree how to help the unemployed and get Germany back on its feet … so they argued … and argued. Two chancellors – Müller and Brüning resigned in quick succession because they couldn't get a majority of politicians to support their ideas. Quite simply, there were so many politicians from so many political parties, that they could never all agree on an appropriate course of action. By 1932, President Hindenburg was having to use his special 'emergency powers' more and more. This meant he didn't even have to consult the democratically elected Reichstag when introducing new laws. In effect then, by 1932, the democratic process in Germany had failed and parties with extreme ideas – like the Nazis and Communists – grew more popular (see **Source D**).

▼ **Source D** *Election results 1928–1932. The numbers show the amount of politicians (or seats) each political party had in the German parliament (Reichstag). Note the steady increase in votes for the Nazis and Communists.*

Party	May 1928	September 1930	July 1932	November 1932
Nazis	12	107	230	196
National	73	41	37	52
People's	45	30	7	11
Centre	62	68	75	70
Democrats	25	20	4	2
Social Democrats	153	143	133	121
Communists	54	77	89	100

FACTOR NO. 3 Fear of Communism

In 1917, there had been a Communist revolution in Russia. The Communist Party took over all businesses, factories and farms. Ordinary Germans, particularly businessmen and farmers, were frightened of the Communists taking over in their own country. Communists didn't believe in religion, so this worried churchgoers too! From the start, Hitler said he'd fight Communism. He sent his own private army, the brownshirted Storm Troopers, to fight with Communist gangs. Hitler gained support from the middle and upper classes (businessmen, landowners, factory owners and so on) because he promised to deal with the Communist threat.

▼ **Source G** *From the BBC series* History File: Nazi Germany, *Episode One.*

"In working-class areas, where the poverty was worst, the Communists attracted six million new members. They called on workers to rise and take over factories, banks and businesses. It had happened in Russia in 1917. The Russian middle class — factory owners, bankers and landowners — had been wiped out and forced to flee abroad. Not surprisingly, most middle-class Germans saw Communism as the worst threat of all … in 1930, Hitler got 6½ million votes. The Nazis, from nowhere, were now the second largest party in the country — the grateful middle class had much to do with it."

FACTOR NO. 4 The personality of Adolf Hitler

Hitler was able to make people believe that he could be trusted to make Germany a great nation. As a powerful and inspiring speaker, he was able to fill his audiences with hope.

▼ **Source H** *A comparison between different classes amongst the ranks of Nazi Party membership in 1930. As you can see, the middle class was incredibly important to the Nazis.*

Category membership	% of Nazi Party	% of German society
Working class	28.1	45.9
Middle class	66.9	35.8
Upper class	5.0	18.3

▼ **Source I** *Jutta Rüdiger, a German worker who lived in Germany in the 1930s, speaking in 1999.*

"I can only explain this. With the desperation and poverty caused by the mass unemployment, it was really terrible. And in this situation, Hitler seemed to be the bringer of salvation [rescue]. He said, 'I will get you out of this misery if you all join in'. And everyone understood."

▼ **Source J** *Adolf Hitler, speaking in July 1932.*

"The German nation will be restored only when the German people find their inner strength once more! … we will rise again, just as our fathers built up Germany."

FACTOR NO. 5 Organisation of the Nazi Party

Hitler thought he could become Germany's ruler by leading armed soldiers in a revolution. He tried this in 1923 but his Munich Putsch failed. In prison, he realised that he needed to change his ideas. He decided to win power legally by winning votes in elections. After prison, Hitler and the Nazis started to spread their ideas.

* Nazi Party offices were set up all over Germany to recruit more loyal followers.

* More newspapers were bought and millions of leaflets and posters were printed (all organised by one of Hitler's most loyal followers, Joseph Goebbels).

* Hitler himself took part in fabulous parades and rallies where he made passionate speeches (again organised by Goebbels).

* The **Hitler Youth Organisation** was set up to encourage younger followers.

After depression hit in the 1930s, the Nazis began to look like the most organised and disciplined group in Germany – the sort of people to restore the nation. Hitler even used new technology in fresh and original ways. In 1932, he used an aeroplane to take him to 20 cities in seven days to make speeches. This, and his constant use of radio, showed how 'in touch' and modern the Nazis were.

FACT *Nearly, but not quite!*

Hitler was confident enough to run for President, Germany's top political post, in 1932. Although Hindenburg won with 19.4 million votes, Hitler's own profile was raised hugely by winning 13.4 million votes. His brilliant campaign provided much needed publicity for Nazi ideas and Hitler decided to channel his energy into securing Germany's second highest political post – Chancellor.

WISE UP WORD

* Hitler Youth Organisation

So when exactly did Hitler become Chancellor?

After the July 1932 election, the Nazis became Germany's most popular political party ... but they didn't have a majority (over half the votes) so President Hindenburg could still give the Chancellor's job to whomever he wanted. Although Hitler demanded to be Chancellor, Hindenburg refused. The President didn't think he could trust him! Instead, Hindenburg appointed an old, experienced politician called Franz von Papen. But von Papen had virtually no support (the people didn't vote for him, remember!) so he called

▲ *Source K* *A Nazi election poster of 1932. The writing means 'Our last hope: Hitler'. Note the different types of people in the poster. Hitler was trying to appeal to different groups in German society. The woman and child are very significant here – Hitler knew he had to secure women's votes and appealed directly to them by realising how badly they were affected by the Depression. Another one of his posters shows a woman standing above her crying child and husband. The caption reads 'Women – save your family and vote for Adolf Hitler'.*

another election. In the November 1932 election, the Nazis remained the most popular party ... but again Hindenburg refused to make Hitler Germany's Chancellor. This time, Hindenburg gave the Chancellor's job to an old friend of his, Kurt von Schleicher. Again, the new Chancellor had no support and wouldn't have been able to make any new laws – so von Schleicher resigned!

Two Chancellors had come and gone in less than a year ... so who was left? On 30 January 1933, Hitler was appointed Chancellor of Germany. Hindenburg and his friends thought they would be able to control him. How wrong they were!

WORK

1 **a** How did each of the following factors help Hitler to become Chancellor in January 1933?
   i)   the Depression
   ii) unhappiness with Weimar democracy
   iii) fear of Communism
   iv) the appeal of Hitler
   v)   organisation of the Nazi Party
  b In your opinion, which was the most important reason? Give reasons for your answer.

2 Look at **Source C**.
  a Make a copy of the graph in your book or work file.
  b In your own words, explain what the graph shows.

3 Look at **Source K**.
  a Who was this election poster designed to appeal to?
  b What does this poster tell us about the tactics used by the Nazis to gain power?

4 Draw a simple cartoon sketch representing each of the following people:
  • a young, unemployed factory worker;
  • a mother of two children;
  • a religious, middle-class businessman;
  • an important member of the German Communist Party;
  • a veteran soldier of the Great War.

Draw a speech bubble next to each sketch. Then explain how each might have reacted to the news that Hitler had become Chancellor.

CLASSIC EXAM QUESTION

How did Hitler become chancellor in 1933?

Hitler takes control

Topic Focus

▸ Hitler went from Chancellor to Supreme Leader of Germany in only 18 months; how did he achieve this?

Exam Focus

▸ To be able to explain the events which lead to Hitler and the Nazis taking full control of Germany.

Adolf Hitler became Chancellor – Prime Minister – of Germany on 30 January 1933. But this didn't mean that Hitler was in complete control. For a start, Hitler owed his job to President Hindenburg. If the President thought Hitler wasn't doing a good enough job, he could sack him and replace him with someone else. Also, Germany was a democracy – so Hitler could only make laws if the Reichstag (German parliament) agreed to them. But more than half the politicians in the Reichstag belonged to political parties *other* than the Nazis.

Remember, the Nazis were getting more votes than any other party – but not the majority of over half the votes they needed to make laws without anyone else's support!

But just 18 months after he became Chancellor, Hitler was a dictator with total power. So how did he do it?

① February 1933

Hitler arranged a new election for March 1933. He hoped he'd win a huge victory and get the majority he wanted in the Reichstag.

As Chancellor, Hitler now controlled most newspapers and radio stations. He also controlled the police who were used to intimidate voters and beat up opponents.

② 27 February 1933

A week before voting day, the Reichstag burned down. A young Communist – Marinus Van der Lubbe – was arrested and blamed for the fire.

Hitler said the fire was part of a Communist plot to take over the country. He said he knew how to deal with the plot.

3 **1 March 1933**

President Hindenburg had the power to make new laws in an emergency – even if the Reichstag didn't agree.

> Just give me the power to deal with Germany's problems.

> Well, there does seem to be a Communist plot - they burned down the Reichstag didn't they?

Hitler persuaded Hindenburg to pass a special 'Protection Law', giving Hitler the power to deal with the 'Communist plot' to take over Germany. Hindenburg agreed.

5 **23 March 1933**

Hitler had stirred up enough fear to persuade politicians in another political party, the Nationalist Party, to join the Nazis. Hitler now had the majority he wanted.

> My new Enabling Act - this gives me the power to do what I want.

Hitler forced the Reichstag to pass the **Enabling Law**.

This gave him the power to make laws *without* asking the rest of the politicians in the Reichstag if they agreed. Now Hitler didn't even have to worry about what Hindenburg thought of him.

4 **March 1933**

The new law – The Law for the Protection of the People and State – banned the leading Communists from taking part in the election campaign. four thousand of them were thrown into prison and all their newspapers were shut down.

> I'm voting Nazi.

> He's the one to deal with the Communists.

> It's Hitler for me.

> That fire was convenient – it's allowed him to ban some of his opponents.

In the election, the Nazis got more votes than ever before – but Hitler still didn't get the majority he wanted.

6 **7 April 1933**

Hitler immediately began to use his new powers.

Nazis were put in charge of all local government, councils and the police. The **Gestapo** (secret police) were formed.

7 **2 May 1933**

Hitler banned all trade unions – he took away their money and threw their leaders in jail.

By removing trade unions, Hitler had taken away a worker's way of complaining about pay and conditions.

9 **2 August 1934**

President Hindenburg died, aged 87.

It's so sad.

This is my chance.

Hitler immediately took over the President's job as well as remaining Chancellor. He made the army swear an oath of loyalty to him too. Hitler decided on the simple title of **Der Führer** – the leader.

8 **14 July 1933**

Hitler banned all political parties in Germany – except the Nazis!

Voting Paper – July 1933	
Put a cross next to who you want to run the country.	
Nazis	☐
People's Party	☐
Centre Party	☐
Democratic Party	☐
Social Democrats	☐
Communists	☐

BANNED

The 'Law Against the Formation of New Parties' stated that anyone trying to set up or run another party would go to prison for three years. Germany was now a one-party state.

▼ **Source A** *Hitler speaking to the Reichstag.*

▼ **Source B** *An illustrator's copy of a cartoon from an American newspaper in February 1936. The caption that goes with it sarcastically says, 'In the last three years, I have restored honour and freedom to the German people.' What is the message of the cartoon?*

▼ **Source C** *The Oath of Loyalty, 1934. Note that the promise is made to Hitler, not Germany. By making all Germany's soldiers say this, Hitler ensured that the only Germans with the power to get rid of him had promised to die for him!*

> "I swear to God that by this sacred oath I will give complete obedience to the Führer, Adolf Hitler … and will be ready as a brave soldier to risk my life at any time for him."

FACT *Who dunnit?*

There have been many theories about what caused the 'Reichstag Fire'. Was it an accident, the work of a mad arsonist or part of a Communist plot? There is also some evidence to suggest the Nazis may have started the fire themselves – then blamed the Communists in order to whip up anti-Communist feeling before an election!

FACT *'The Night of the Long Knives'*

The SA – the brownshirted Storm Troopers – had been Hitler's private army of thugs since 1921. This tough group of men, who protected Nazi meetings, drummed up support and attacked opponents, was now a force of four million men. The SA leader, Ernst Roehm, wanted them to join the army. The army didn't want 'these thieves, drunks and sods' as they called them. Hitler worried that Roehm could call on the SA to get rid of him. At 3:00am on 30 June 1934, hundreds of regional SA leaders – and Roehm – were arrested on Hitler's orders, taken to prison … and shot dead. The murders were committed by Hitler's own black-shirted **SS** guards, who were fiercely loyal to him. The SA was finished – and the whole incident became known as the **Night of the Long Knives**.

WISE UP WORDS

- Night of the Long Knives   Enabling Law   Führer
  Gestapo   SS

WORK

1   Explain how Hitler was able to increase his power on each of the following dates: 27 February 1933; 1 March 1933; 23 March 1933; 7 April 1933; 2 May 1933; 14 July 1933; 30 June 1934; 2 August 1934. Present your work in a table; the first one has been done for you:

DATE	EVENT	HOW IT INCREASED HITLER'S POWER
27th February 1933	The Reichstag burned down	With 'evidence' of a Communist plot, Hitler was able to go to Hindenburg and try to get him to ban the Communist Party.
1st March 1933		

2   Look at **Source A**.

   a The meeting photographed here does not look like a parliament meeting as we know it. In what ways does the layout of the hall make discussion difficult?

   b How does the decoration of the hall support Hitler's dictatorship?

3   Look at **Source B**. What point is the cartoonist making about Hitler's control of Germany?

CLASSIC EXAM QUESTION

- Describe the main features of the Enabling Act.
- Why did the Night of the Long Knives take place?
- How was Hitler able to increase his power between January 1933 and August 1934?

Have you been learning?

TASK 1 Note-making

Note-making is an important skill. To do it successfully, you must pick out key words or phrases in sentences. These key words and phrases are vital to the meaning of the sentence – without them, the sentence makes no sense.

For example: Hitler joined the German army when the Great War started in 1914. He won several medals for bravery doing the very difficult job of carrying messages around the trenches. By the time the war ended, he had even managed to win the Iron Cross (First Class), which was the highest bravery award in the German army. (56 words)

The key words and phrases are: Hitler, joined German army, 1914, bravery medals, carrying messages in trenches, won Iron Cross (First Class), highest bravery award. (19 words)

Now write down the key words and phrases from the following paragraphs. Each one is about Germany in the 1920s. The key words and phrases will be your notes.

a The 1920s have been called a 'golden age' for German artists, writers, poets and performers. Before the Great War, the Kaiser kept tight control on all types of entertainment – now he was gone, the German people felt a new sense of freedom. After the horrors of the Great War, people decided to experiment with new ideas and try new things.

b The 1920s were a golden age for German cinema. *Metropolis*, directed by the famous Fritz Lang, was the most technically advanced film of the decade, whilst Marlene Dietrich became a worldwide star playing glamorous, strong-willed women.

c Germany became a centre for new plays, operas and theatre shows in the 1920s. Bertolt Brecht's *Threepenny Opera* was a box office smash hit. Cabaret artists performed songs that criticised politicians and would have been banned in the Kaiser's day. There were songs about sex too, which shocked older Germans.

d Writing became big business in Germany too. People had 120 newspapers and magazines to choose from and one anti-war novel, *All Quiet on the Western Front*, by Erich Remarque sold half a million copies in just three months. It has since been turned into two highly successful films.

e Art flourished in Germany as well. 'Modern artists' such as Otto Dix and George Grosz used their art to criticise some of the things they saw happening in Germany. They painted the stark differences between the richer, fashionable people in the nightclubs and the poor beggars on the streets who had fought in the war and returned home with missing limbs or shattered minds.

Big city by Otto Dix

f Some Germans hated these cultural changes. They wanted art, music, theatre, film and literature to celebrate older, traditional values and hated this new period of experimentation. They thought the 'new era' was leading Germany into a moral decline.

TASK 2 Cartoon time

Study this cartoon carefully. It was published in Britain in 1919 and comments on the Treaty of Versailles.

DER TAG!

a Which country is represented by the man on the left being strangled by a large hand?

b Who do you think the four men holding the spoon are?

c What are the four men attempting to feed the man on the left?

d What point do you think the cartoonist was trying to make about the Treaty of Versailles?

TASK 3 Unscramble the scramble

Here is a mixed-up set of dates and names – and the places connected with them. Your task is to unscramble them, put them into groups of three and then explain the connections between them. One has been done for you.

November 1923   Wolfgang Kapp   February 1919
Adolf Hitler   Friedrich Ebert   November 1918
Spartacists   Weimar   Berlin   Treaty of Versailles
Paris   Kaiser Wilhelm II   Munich   June 1919
Berlin   Holland   January 1919   March 1920

Example:

DATE	NAME	PLACE	CONNECTION
November 1918	Kaiser Wilhelm II	Holland	By the beginning of **November 1918**, Germany was in chaos. There were riots and strikes. **Kaiser Wilhelm II** had lost control and gave up his throne. He secretly left Germany for **Holland**, never to return.

TASK 4 Question time

Look at these genuine GCSE questions carefully. Why not try to complete one, two or even all of them as a revision exercise? In brackets after each question, you will find the pages of this book where there is information that might refresh your memory.

- Why did most Germans hate the Treaty of Versailles? (pages 12 and 13)

- Describe the Spartacus Uprising of 1919. (pages 8 and 9)

- What was the Free Corps? (pages 8 and 9)

- What were Hitler's main beliefs? (pages 22 to 25)

- Why did the Munich (Beer Hall) Putsch fail? (pages 24 and 25)

- Explain why the Nazis had not got into power by 1928. (pages 22 to 27)

- The following were factors that threatened the Weimar Republic in 1923:

  i) the French invasion of the Ruhr;

  ii) the inflation of the mark;

  iii) the Munich (Beer Hall) Putsch.

Which of these factors do you think was the greatest threat? Explain your answer, referring to i, ii and iii only. (pages 14 to 17)

- Did Stresemann succeed in solving the problems faced by the Weimar Republic? (pages 26 and 27)

- Was the Weimar Republic a complete failure? Explain your answer. (pages 14 to 17)

- How did Hitler develop the Nazi Party between 1924 and 1932? (pages 30 to 33)

What sort of learner are you?

Lots of recent research has suggested that people learn in different ways – in other words, all of us have a **preferred learning style**. Although there are lots of different ways to learn, in recent years experts have narrowed it down to three key styles: Visual, Auditory and Kinaesthetic (VAK). In many schools today, teachers have worked hard to make students aware of their preferred learning style – and it is fairly easy to go online, answer a few short questions and work out whether you are mainly a visual, auditory or kinaesthetic learner. However, for those students who have no idea what their preferred learning style is, the chart below may help you out.

Do you like...?	Possible preferred learning style
Seeing, reading, learning by looking at diagrams, demonstrations, displays, handouts, films, charts etc., using highlighters to colour-code.	Visual 
Listening, speaking, learning by copying down information from DVDs, podcasts or TV, discussing things with friends after just learning them, saying things over and over again until they 'sink in'.	Auditory 
Touching, doing, learning by creating imaginative charts, grids and timelines, re-enacting situations, cutting things up and rearranging them on the page, visits for understanding.	Kinaesthetic 

Knowing your preferred learning style will help you revise for your exams. It should help you focus your revision in a way most suited to help you learn and retain the most information.

Look carefully at the targeted revision techniques detailed on these pages. Once you have worked out your preferred learning style, try to use some of the techniques when revising.

*If you are a **visual** learner...*

- Try to put your notes into particular categories.
- Organise your notes in to sections – try colour coding them – perhaps write the key facts in a bold colour.
- Draw pictures or find photos from the internet to accompany your notes
- Write the things you need to remember on wall charts and on posters to hang around your bedroom.
- It will help you if memorise various parts of your note-taking.
- Use colour-coded index cards to help you to organise your revision by concentrating on one colour set each night.
- Use video clips to help you remember the facts you need to know, making notes as you watch.

*If you are an **auditory** learner...*

- Very often it is important to discuss your revision with friends, talk about the things you have just learned and understand.
- It is easier sometimes to do your homework with other students who are also auditory learners.
- Record your own revision onto tape or your iPod and play it back to yourself.
- It is important to say information over and over in order to retain it.
- If possible act out or tell a story about various things you need to remember from your studies. You will then be able to imagine the story you have created in your head when writing it down in an exam.
- Sometimes it could help to try to make up a rhyme about what you are trying to remember, you could also try to put it to a tune.
- Try studying in a group, this might help you to learn.
- Use background music to help you concentrate.

*If you are a **kinaesthetic** learner...*

- Copy things out over and over again making them neat and presented in an organised fashion.
- Visit as many places linked to your studies as possible.
- Wherever possible try to trace the key words you need to remember with your hand or finger.
- Try to construct things whilst you are studying e.g. a model to help you learn.
- Create flash cards to help prompt you when learning.
- Take frequent breaks when you are studying.
- Use memory techniques using hand gestures to help you to remember.
- Don't read large amounts of text at any one time – you will not take 50% of it in.

TOP EXAM TIP

Don't use just the one revision style to get your brain really buzzing, use a variety of techniques.

Studying Sources Made Simple

Many of your history lessons over the years will have featured **SOURCES** in some way. Quite simply a source is a piece of information. A source can be a document, a painting, a photograph, poster, chart, diary entry, speech, even a set of statistics ... in fact anything that provides us with information. In your exam you will almost certainly be asked questions about any number of sources that appear on the exam paper in front of you. The sources might be posters, cartoons, advertisements, diagrams, photographs, paintings, maps or charts. They could be speeches by famous politicians, quotes from old textbooks or opinions of historians written in modern magazine articles.

There are five main types of source question – and your first job when confronted with a source question is to work out what type of question it is!

Source question type 1: Extraction

An EXTRACTION question challenges the student to get as much out of the source as they can.

Typical questions:

- What can we learn from Sources A and B about ... ?
- What does Source D tell us about... ?

Top tips

- Make sure you understand the source – read it slowly and carefully, including the label (or provenance, as it is sometimes known)
- Write down what the source tells us about the specific issue asked in the question. For example, if you are asked what a source tells us about the way Hitler used the Great Depression to gain support – make sure you write down at least three things that the source tells you
- Try to write down what you can infer from the source. For example, is there a message in the source? Is it trying to create an impression by trying to make you think in a certain way?
- Also, what does the source tell you about the author, the time it was written and/or the situation in which it was written?

Source question type 2: Similarities and differences

A SIMILARITY/DIFFERENCE question asks a student to compare and contrast a number of sources

Typical questions:

- Do the sources agree about... ?
- In what way do Sources A and B differ about... ?
- Why is Source A's interpretation different to Source B's?

Top tips

- If asked HOW two sources are similar or different, look for basic things to compare – mention what they agree on for example, and what they disagree on! Also look for differences and/or similarities in tone, approach, message etc.
- If asked WHY the sources are similar or different, you need to look carefully at the label that accompanies the source. Look who wrote it, and when, and in what context or situation. Think why it was written and for what purpose.
- Wherever possible here, use quotes from the sources to back up the point you are trying to make ... and write a conclusion to your answer too, summing up how and/or why they are similar or different.

Source question type 3: Reliability

RELIABILITY questions want students to judge how accurate and reliable a source is.

Typical questions:

- How accurate is Source C as a source of information... ?
- How reliable is... ?

Top tips

- Try to establish the extent to which the source might be biased or exaggerated. Look at the words, phrases and language. Use your own knowledge here – does the source give you an accurate picture of things? Compare it to other sources that might be available.

- Look at the label to establish who wrote it and when. Try to judge how one sided or exaggerated it might be. Think whether it gives the whole story and point out, from your own knowledge, what it misses out! Is the writer trying to 'make a point' for example? Do they have a reason or motive to lie?

- Make sure you come to a conclusion here, based on facts. And try to avoid general phrases like 'it is biased' without backing it up with evidence. For example write 'it would be biased because ...' instead.

Source question type 5: Final conclusions

Exam papers often include CONCLUSION questions which ask students to use all the sources. The question often asks students to debate a particular issue, or proposition, and use the sources to back up their conclusion.

Typical questions:

- Use all the sources to debate...
- Do all the sources agree that public health improved at different times for different reasons?

Top tips

- Look through all the sources again with the question in mind.
- The sources have been selected to support both sides of the argument, or position. Use them to argue both for and against, making sure you take into account the accuracy and reliability of the sources you use to reach your conclusion.

Source question type 4: Utility

UTILITY questions ask how useful a source is. 'Utility' is just another way of asking how 'useful' a source is to a historian studying that particular period of time.

Typical question:

- How useful is Source D as evidence about how Hitler and the Nazis dealt with opposition?

Top tips

- Utility questions are all about QUANTITY and QUALITY – how much information does it give you, and how reliable is that information? The most reliable source, therefore, is one that tells you a lot and you can trust what it says!

- Think about what the source tells you ... and think whether it's actually the sort of information you're looking for in relation to the question.

- Look at the sufficiency of the source – does it give you the whole story? Explain the source's limitations – as well as explaining what it is used for.

- Think about who produced it, why, and whether you can trust them. If you can trust a source – you must explain why! And just because a source is widely inaccurate in what it says, doesn't mean it isn't useful – it perhaps reveals a lot about the author's feelings, prejudices and opinions. In fact, nothing is ever useless, no matter how biased it is. Remember that the source reveals lots about the individual or the government of the organisation that produces it.

FACT *Think SOURCE when evaluating one*

Source – Where is it from? When was it written? Who is the author?

Objective –Why was it written? For a diary, a newspaper, a speech?

Usefulness – What use is it for the question you are answering?

Reliability – Can you trust it? If so why/why not?

Context – What was going on at the time it was written? Put the source into context. Use your background knowledge here.

Example – Always use an example from the source to back up what you have written.

How did the Nazis control Germany?

Topic Focus

▶ These pages will help you to remember how Hitler controlled ordinary Germans' support.

Exam Focus

▶ To know at least two examples of Nazi control and the ways in which the Nazis controlled the media.

The vast majority of Germans supported Hitler and the Nazis throughout the 1930s (or at least they said they did!). Like a pop star or celebrity footballer today, Hitler was mobbed wherever he went as thousands of people turned up to catch a glimpse of him and chant his name. He received dozens of marriage proposals every month and outside his house in southern Germany, some visitors even went so far as to eat the gravel where he'd stood! As you might expect, the Nazis faced little opposition in the 1930s. So what did they do to make sure of this? Why were ordinary Germans so keen to let the Nazis continue to run their country? In short, how did the Nazis keep control?

The Nazis used a range of methods to control Germany. Read about each method carefully. Your task at the end of these four pages is to answer a genuine GCSE question from a popular examination board.

METHOD 1: Terror

Some people went along with the Nazis simply because they were too scared to speak out against them. They didn't necessarily support Hitler but feared the consequences of objecting to him. Special organisations even existed to terrorise people into accepting Nazi rule.

The man in charge of all aspects of 'Nazi terror' was Heinrich Himmler, a loyal Nazi who had known Hitler since 1923.

Heinrich Himmler

Job description
SS Gestapo
concentration camps

Gestapo

The secret police were known as the Gestapo. Their job was to crush anyone who was against Hitler. They spied on people they thought were a threat, tapped telephone lines and opened mail. They had the power to arrest, imprison without trial and torture anyone. They set up a huge network of informers who would report any 'grumblers' to them. Even children were encouraged to report their parents or teachers if they moaned or made an anti-Hitler joke.

The police and law courts

The ordinary police continued their regular work but ignored most crimes committed by Nazis. The law courts were under Nazi control too. New laws meant that the death penalty could be given for, among other things, telling an anti-Nazi joke, having sex with a Jew or listening to a foreign radio station.

The SS

SS stands for 'Schutz Staffel', which means 'protection squad'. Set up in 1925, the SS were originally Hitler's private bodyguards. Gradually, it was built up to be the most important armed group in Germany. SS members were tall, fit, blond-haired and blue-eyed. You couldn't even become a member if you'd had a tooth filled! Mainly, the SS had three sections: one section looked after security – they could arrest anybody without good reason and search houses. Another section was the Waffen SS – providing elite units in the army. The final section was the Death's Head Units – they ran the concentration camps and, later, the death camps.

Source A This photograph shows Heinrich Himmler visiting one of his dreaded **concentration camps**.

Source B From a modern history textbook.

"Imagine that you are German, that you are walking along a street in Germany and that you recognise a group of people walking towards you. This is what a German newspaper of 1936 said you should do:

'...raise the right arm at an angle so that the palm of the hand becomes visible. The appropriate phrase that goes with it is "Heil Hitler" or at least "Heil" ... the greeting should always be carried out with the left arm if one's right arm is held by a lady.'

If you are the kind of person who likes a quiet life, you will always follow these rules when you see people you know: there is always a chance that one of them will report you to the Gestapo if you do not give the 'German greeting'."

Concentration camps

Lots of these were set up as soon as Hitler took power. They were like large prisons where any 'enemies of the German state' could be held for any length of time. Anyone the Nazis didn't like was sent there – Jews, homosexuals, gypsies, old political opponents and anyone who had criticised Hitler. Inmates were forced to work hard and listen to Nazi ideas all day long. Some were even tortured or worked to death.

METHOD 2: Propaganda

Hitler knew that he didn't have to terrorise all Germans – many supported Hitler and the Nazis because they thought they were doing an excellent job. However, to make sure as many people as possible realised how great the Nazis were, Hitler put someone in charge of what is known as **propaganda**.

Propaganda comes from the word 'propagate'. Propagate means 'to spread information and ideas'. Hitler employed a leading Nazi named Joseph Goebbels to persuade large numbers of Germans to think what Hitler wanted them to think and believe what Hitler wanted them to believe. Goebbels was brilliant at his job.

Films

- All film plots were shown to Goebbels before films were made.
- All films had to show Nazis in a good way – and their 'enemies' in a bad way.

CLASSIC EXAM QUESTION

How did Hitler keep control?

Radio

- The Nazis controlled all radio stations – they were used to put across Nazi ideas.
- Cheap radios were produced – more Germans owned radios in the 1930s than Americans.
- Loudspeakers were placed in the streets, in factories and cafes.

Newspapers

- Goebbels told newspapers what they could print – only stories that showed the Nazis doing good things were printed.
- Newspapers that printed new stories that Goebbels hadn't seen were closed down.

The Ministry of Enlightenment and Propaganda

Dr Joseph Goebbels.

Mass rallies

- Spectacular parades – called **mass rallies** – were held every year to celebrate Hitler's greatness – special arenas were built that could hold half a million people. They listened to choirs, bands, speeches and watched firework displays and air shows. All were designed to show how impressive and well organised the Nazis were.

Books, theatre and music

- Writers were forced to write books and plays that praised Hitler and the Nazis.
- Books written by Jews, Communists or anti-Nazi journalists were banned – in Berlin in 1933, students burned 20 000 books in a public bonfire.
- Jazz music was banned throughout Germany because it originated among the black people of America.

▼ **Source E** *An instruction, given by Goebbels, to all newspapers in 1934.*

"In the next issue of your newspaper there will be a main article about a decision made by Hitler. No matter what his decision is, you will write that it is the only correct one for Germany."

WISE UP WORDS

- mass rally   propaganda
  concentration camps

WORK

1   Here are six real-life situations. In your opinion, do you think each person is being controlled by: i) terror; ii) propaganda; iii) a combination of the two?

   Briefly describe each situation and then write out how you think the person is being controlled or why they acted in the way they did:

a   An important church leader is imprisoned for speaking out against the Nazis.

b   A famous musician and his family flee from Germany because they are Jews and fear the Nazis.

c   A woman in Munich donates money to the Nazi Party because she is impressed by one of Hitler's speeches.

d   A young student burns some of his books because he refuses to read anything written by a Jew.

e   A teacher gives the Nazi salute every morning to each of his classes, even though he hates Hitler.

f   An eight-year-old boy informs his head teacher that his father keeps telling anti-Hitler jokes which are banned.

2   This is a genuine GCSE question.

   'Propaganda was the most important reason for the lack of opposition in Nazi Germany'. Do you agree with this statement? Explain your answer carefully.

▲ **Source C** *A mass rally in Nuremberg, 1937.*

▼ **Source D** *Adapted from Hitler's book, Mein Kampf, written in 1924.*

"The powers of ordinary people to understand are weak. And they quickly forget. So good propaganda has to be limited to a very few points. These must be as simple as possible and the slogans must be repeated until everybody has come to grasp the idea."

Hitler the demagogue

Exam Focus

▶ You will need to understand the power of Hitler's speeches and why what he said, and how he said it, appealed to the masses.

A **demagogue** is a political leader who appeals to the prejudice and passions of huge numbers of ordinary people. Without any doubt, Hitler had the rare gift of being able to arouse almost fanatical support through the power of his speeches. So how did he do it? Why is Hitler known as one of the greatest speakers the world has ever seen?

▼ **Source A** *Hitler, pictured in 1936, about to give one of his famous speeches.*

▼ **Source B** *A modern historian describes Hitler's voice.*

"His booming voice, hypnotic eyes and fearful temper thrilled his audiences. One expert calculated that the frequency of an angry man's voice is 200 vibrations per second. The frequency of Hitler's normal speaking voice was 228 vibrations per second. One historian described his voice as an 'assault on the eardrums'."

▼ **Source C** *Otto Strasser, a Nazi who disliked Hitler, writing about his skills as a public speaker.*

"He is one of the greatest speakers of the century. Adolf Hitler enters. He sniffs the air. For a minute he gropes, feels his way, senses the atmosphere. Suddenly he bursts forth. His words go like an arrow to their target, telling the crowd what it most wants to hear."

▼ **Source D** *A German woman speaking in the 1930s.*

"For years, it was my wish to meet him. I knew his voice from the radio. I saw his picture every day — on my father's desk and on my wall next to my bed. I felt that I would only be satisfied if I could meet him once.

But when I saw him I wanted more. I wanted to see him close up: I wanted to hear him speak, to shake his hand. I wanted to tell him something, to thank him. But I would not have been able to say a word; like so many young and old, in those days, I would have only wept."

▼ **Source E** *Karl Ludeckm, an early follower of Hitler, remembers the first time he heard Hitler speak.*

"He was holding the masses and me with them, under a hypnotic spell … I do not know how to describe the emotions that swept over me as I heard this man. His words were like a whip. When he spoke of the disgrace of Germany, I felt ready to spring on any enemy."

▼ **Source F** *Written by a leading Nazi, Kurt Ludecke in 1932.*

"…more than a hundred thousand had paid to see him … and at home, millions were waiting by the radio… Suddenly a wave surged over the crowd … Hitler is coming! Hitler is coming! A blow of trumpets fill the air and a hundred thousand people leap to their feet … all eyes were turned forward awaiting their Führer. There was a low rumble of excitement and then the crowd burst into a tremendous ovation, the 'Heils' swelling until they were like the roar of a mighty waterfall."

▼ **Source G** *Joseph Goebbels.*

"His blue eyes met my glance like a flame. This was a command. Now I know which road to take."

WISE UP WORD

- demagogue

WORK

1 a Write out a dictionary definition of the word 'demagogue'.

 b Why is demagogue such a suitable word to describe Adolf Hitler? Give reasons for your answer.

2 Look carefully at **Sources C**, **D**, **E**, **F** and **G**. Each of these people actually met Hitler or heard him speak. If you could ask the writer of each source to describe Adolf Hitler using no more than five words, write down what they might say.

Hitler's image

Topic Focus

▸ These pages will help you to understand how Hitler manufactured his image in order to maintain his popularity.

Exam Focus

▸ Describe the different ways Hitler used to portray himself.
▸ What message did these different techniques send to the German people?

One of Hitler's greatest achievements was the way in which he managed to maintain his popularity for so long. The first political leader to have a totally manufactured image, Adolf Hitler made expert use of paintings, photographs and posters to hypnotise a whole nation. So what sort of image was he trying to promote?

The children's friend

▸ **Source B**

Hitler was always keen to be photographed with children. Here he is pictured receiving flowers in 1940.

Stop and think: why do you think Hitler felt it was important to be photographed with children as much as possible?

▾ **Source C** *Comment by G. Ward-Price, writing in the Daily Mail in 1937. Most historians agree that Hitler's love of children and dogs was genuine – he didn't just like them 'for the cameras'.*

"He looks healthy, his skin fresh and his pale blue eyes bright. Fondness for children and dogs is a strong part of Hitler's character."

The brave leader

▾ **Source A**

Hitler commissioned this poster in 1934. It is called 'Long Live Germany'.

Stop and think: why is Hitler painted in front of so many men? Why do you think so many swastika flags are included in the picture? What sort of expression had the artist tried to paint on Hitler's face? Why have light beams been shown shining down on Hitler? Why have Hitler's medals been included in the painting?

Mr Popular

▸ **Source D**

This photograph was taken in 1937. It shows dozens of people looking adoringly at their leader.

Stop and think: why do you think Hitler thought this was an excellent photograph and ordered it to be shown all over Germany?

Hitler worked hard to appeal to women too.

Stop and think: despite having a girlfriend, Eva Braun, for many years, why do you think Hitler ordered that her existence should be kept secret from the German people?

▾ **Source E** *Adolf Hitler, speaking in 1938. Stop and think: do you agree with Hitler – are women more attracted to unmarried film stars and celebrities?*

> "Lots of women are attracted to me because I'm unmarried. It's the same with a film star."

WORK

1 Why was Hitler's image so important to the Nazis?

2 **a** Look at each of the photographs on these pages (**Sources A**, **B**, **D** and **F**). For each one, explain what impression it gives you of Hitler.

   b Why do you think **Source F** was censored?

   c Imagine you work in Germany in 1936 and have been given the job of choosing a photograph to go on the front of a new book about Hitler's life. The four pictures on these pages have been short-listed. Which picture would you choose? Give reasons for your answer.

3 Look at **Source G**.

   a Albert Speer worked for Hitler, who regarded Speer as a close friend. Do you think Speer's book was published during or after Hitler's time as leader of Germany? Give reasons for your answer.

   b In what ways does Speer's account contradict Hitler's public image?

The hard worker

▾ **Source F**

Hitler was presented as a leader who worked very hard for the German people. The photograph in **Source F**, *showing Hitler at work, was never seen by the German people because it shows Hitler wearing glasses (which he needed for reading). He preferred to be pictured without his glasses so the picture was censored (as shown by the cross).*

Stop and think: why didn't Hitler want people to see him in his glasses?

▾ **Source G** *Adapted from the book* Inside the Third Reich *by Albert Speer, the official Nazi architect.*

> "He got up late in the morning and had one or two meetings. After dinner, he just wasted time until the evening. His rare appointments in the later afternoon were ruined because he always loved to look at building plans. The assistants in his office asked me: 'Please don't leave any plans today…' In the eyes of the people, Hitler was the leader who watched over the nation day and night. This was hardly so."

Who was on Hitler's hate list?

Topic Focus

▸ These pages will help you to understand why the Nazis persecuted the Jews, as well as other minority and racial groups.

Exam Focus

▸ To be able to explain 'anti-Semitism' and describe some of the persecution the Jews suffered and why it got gradually worse from 1933 to 1939.

Having worked hard to get into power, Hitler was determined to remove any possible threats. He said he would crush anyone who didn't fully support him, declaring that those Germans who spoke out against him would 'have their skulls bashed in'. Some of Hitler's first targets therefore were his old political opponents. During Hitler's first few months in power, dozens of people who had belonged to any political party other than the Nazis found themselves sent to new tough prisons known as concentration camps. But other groups in German society found themselves high on Hitler's hate list too, despite not appearing to be any threat to his power at all! So why did Hitler **persecute** certain racial groups? And who were the so-called 'undesirables' that Hitler was so determined to remove?

The persecution of racial groups

Hitler believed that some races were better – or **superior** – to others. He felt that a 'master race' (like the Germans) had the right to dominate **inferior** races, such as Jews, Gypsies, Slavs (such as Russians), black and Indian people. Hitler used the word Aryan to describe the master race of Germans he planned. Ideally, an Aryan would be tall, strong, blond, blue-eyed … and white! Hitler feared that his Aryans would mix with some of the so-called inferior groups so the Nazis began to persecute and, later, murder them. Over half a million Gypsies died in death camps in the years up to 1945 … and over six million Jews from all over Europe!

▸ **Source A** Each of these laws was designed to drive Jews out of Germany. There were approximately 500 000 Jews in Germany in 1934 (about 1% of the population). By the time Hitler stopped Jews leaving Germany (1941), nearly 80% had left for new lives in other countries. From 1941 onwards, Hitler began his **'Final Solution'** to kill all of Europe's Jews.

TOP EXAM TIP

Anti-Semitism means hatred of Jewish people. It had existed in Europe for hundred of years, occasionally boiling over into violent 'pogroms' (violent racial attacks).

LAWS AGAINST JEWS, 1933–1939

March 1933 All Jewish lawyers and judges sacked.

April 1933 All Jews banned from any sports clubs. All Jewish teachers sacked.

September 1933 'Race studies' introduced in German schools.

January 1934 All Jewish shops marked with a yellow star of David – a symbol of the Jewish religion – or the word *Juden* (German for 'Jew'). Soldiers to stand outside shops turning people away.

September 1935 Jews not allowed to vote. Marriages between Jews and non-Jews banned. These were known as the **Nuremberg Laws**.

January 1936 No Jew allowed to own any electrical equipment (including cameras), bicycles, typewriters or music records.

July 1938 Jewish doctors sacked.

August 1938 Male Jews must add the name 'Israel' and female Jews must add the name 'Sara' to their first names.

November 1938 Jewish children banned from German schools.

December 1938 Jewish and non-Jewish children forbidden to play together. Jews banned from using swimming pools.

April 1939 Jews can be evicted from their homes for no reason.

September 1939 Jews no longer allowed out of their homes between 8:00pm and 6:00am.

▼ **_Source B_** *A Jewish family are forced to leave their home town as Nazis laugh and jeer in the background.*

The persecution of 'undesirables'

Hitler believed that every single German should work to make Germany a greater nation. There were certain groups, he felt, that were incapable of this and that their existence weakened the nation. Hitler called these people 'undesirable' and wanted to get rid of them in order to strengthen Germany.

* Around half a million tramps, beggars and alcoholics were sent to concentration camps in 1933. Many were worked to death. Hitler believed that these people offered nothing to his nation.

* Thousands of prostitutes, homosexuals and problem families were sent to the camps too. Hitler believed that ideal Germans were married, had lots of children and created a secure, loving home ... and these three groups did not do what he wanted!

* Many people with strong religious beliefs were sent to the camps. Some were **pacifists** who refused to go into the army. Others, like Jehovah's Witnesses, for example, refused to offer total loyalty to anyone other than God. Hitler hated this, as he wanted all Germans to be totally loyal to him and fight for him if needed, so he sent hundreds of them to the concentration camps.

* About 350 000 physically and mentally disabled men and women were forcibly **sterilised** by the Nazis. They just didn't fit in with Hitler's vision of a race of strong and powerful Aryans so he wanted to stop them passing on any of their 'deformities' to their children. From 1939, the Nazis began to kill them. About 200 000 people, including 5000 children, were murdered in specially built 'nursing homes'.

▼ **_Source C_** *Based on an interview with a former prisoner of one of Hitler's concentration camps.*

"The prisons were full. Tramps, prostitutes and beggars were a common sight, but there were other prisoners too. Anyone who refused to join the army was sent to prison and so were people who'd been a member of any other political party except the Nazis. Trade union leaders were also inside and I once met a woman who had been reported for telling a joke at the Führer's expense. Another favourite tactic of the Gestapo was to accuse a man or woman of being homosexual — there were many in prison accused of this 'crime'."

WISE UP WORDS

* pacifist   persecute   inferior   superior
  Nuremberg Laws   Final Solution   sterilisation

WORK

1 **a** Write out a dictionary definition of the word 'persecute'.

   b Explain why Hitler felt he had the right to persecute certain racial groups.

2 Look at **Source A**. Explain which of the restrictions:

   i) were annoying or minor nuisances;

   ii) prevented Jewish children from having a normal childhood;

   iii) prevented Jews from earning a normal living;

   iv) prevented Jews from enjoying the same rights as other German citizens.

3 Between 1933 and 1941, nearly 80% of Jewish families left Germany for new lives in other countries. Make up a conversation between two Jewish families – one determined to leave, the other determined to stay. Think about what factors will be influencing their decision.

4 Why did Hitler regard each of the following as 'undesirable' in Nazi Germany?

   i) prostitutes

   ii) homosexuals

   iii) tramps

   iv) pacifists

What happened at Hartheim Castle?

Topic Focus

▶ To understand what Operation T-4 was, and how ordinary Germans and the Catholic church showed their disapproval of it.

Exam Focus

▶ Be able to explain why Hitler and the Nazis began Operation T-4, and what they believed its purpose to be.

Hartheim Castle, near Linz in Austria, was once the private home of several Austrian princes. In 1898, the castle was donated to charity and became a home for physically and mentally disabled children. Forty-two years later, the Nazis were using most of the ground floor of Hartheim Castle Children's Home as a huge gas chamber to murder thousands of men, women and children. So why was this taking place? Who authorised the killings? And what exactly happened at Hartheim Castle?

Hitler passionately believed that certain groups in society would damage the purity of his 'master race' if they were allowed to have children. He thought that certain 'defective' people should be prevented from 'breeding' in case they passed on their 'deformities'. In July 1933, he passed a law that stated that anyone who suffered from 'feeble mindedness, depression, serious physical disability, blindness, deafness or were seriously alcoholic' could be forced to have an operation that prevented them from having children (sterilisation). In total, approximately 300 000 men and women were sterilised between 1933 and 1939. In 1939, Hitler decided to go a step further and introduce the T-4 **euthanasia** programme.

On 1 September 1939, Hitler signed an order giving Nazi doctors the power to 'administer a mercy death to the incurably sick' – in other words, an official government euthanasia programme. It was named T-4 after the address of the building in Berlin – Tiergartenstrasse 4 – from where the programme was organised. Any baby or toddler identified as physically or mentally disabled by a doctor, nurse or midwife would be taken from their family and put in a special children's ward in one of 20 hospitals. In these wards, health care workers killed at least 5000 children through lethal injection or starvation! Soon the T-4 programme was extended to adults and six killing centres were created where the disabled were murdered in gas chambers and their bodies burned (see **Source C**). Hartheim Castle was one of these special T-4 killing centres created in Austria a year after Hitler's Germany took over the country in 1938. In all, 'Operation T-4' claimed at least 200 000 lives.

▼ **Source A** *Hartheim Castle.*

THIS PERSON SUFFERING FROM HEREDITARY DEFECTS COSTS THE PEOPLE 60 000 REICHSMARK DURING HIS LIFETIME. PEOPLE, THAT IS YOUR MONEY.

▲ **Source B** *A poster from 1936 that attempts to justify the compulsory sterilisation programme. 'Hereditary' means passed on from one family generation to the next.*

▼ **Source C** *A modern historian writes about what happened at Hartheim Castle.*

"The killing installation occupied the ground floor of the castle ... it included a series of rooms for receiving, examining and undressing patients, a gas chamber that was disguised as a shower room and at least two crematoria. After the victims were gassed, their gold teeth were extracted. Then their bodies were burned and their bones pulverised in a bone mill. At least once a week a truck carried the remains to the Danube river, where it was dumped into the water."

FACT *Not so popular!*

'Operation T-4' was heavily criticised in Germany, especially by important Church leaders. In December 1940, the Pope himself issued a statement condemning euthanasia (although he didn't mention 'Operation T-4' itself). During August 1941, Hitler's personal train was delayed near Nuremberg whilst some disabled patients were loaded onto trucks bound for a T-4 killing centre. A brave crowd gathered to jeer and boo at Hitler during the delay. On 18 August 1941, Hitler publicly ordered a halt to 'Operation T-4' ... but told leading Nazis to continue with the programme in secret!

WISE UP WORDS

• euthanasia   hereditary

WORK

1 Test your understanding of this unit by writing a sentence or two about these words:

sterilisation • euthanasia • hereditary

2 **a** What was Operation T-4?

   b Why was Operation T-4 started?

   c What do you think about Operation T-4?

3 Look at **Source B**. Why do you think the Nazis ordered posters like this to appear in newspapers and magazines all over Germany?

4 **a** Working in pairs, imagine you both live in Germany in the late 1930s and know all about Operation T-4. One of you should be pro-Nazi, the other anti-Nazi. In no more than 50 words, write down your opinion of Operation T-4.

   b In what ways are your opinions different?

'Work and bread'

Topic Focus

▶ To remember at least two ways the Nazis cut unemployment after 1933.

Over six million Germans were out of work when Hitler came to power in 1933. In his election campaigns, he had promised the voters 'work and bread' if he became their leader (see **Source A**). Now he had to find them jobs. So how did the Nazis get Germans back to work?

▼ **Source A** *A Nazi election poster from 1932.*

▼ **Source B** *The rise and fall of unemployment in Germany, 1929–1939.*

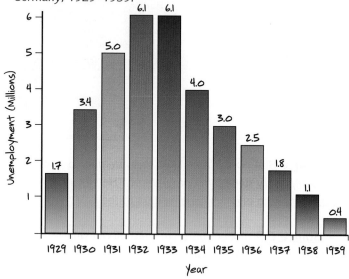

CLASSIC EXAM QUESTION

In what ways did Hitler attempt to solve Germany's economic problems?

The National Labour Service (Reichsarbeitsdienst or RAD) was set up

All men aged between 18 and 25 had to spend six months in the RAD. They planted forests and built motorways (autobahns), hospitals and schools. Men in the RAD had to wear uniforms and live in camps but they were given free meals. They were paid only pocket money but at least it was a job ... and the unemployment figures dropped rapidly!

Hitler introduced conscription

From 1935, all males aged between 18 and 25 were forced to join the army, navy or air force for at least two years. In just five years, the army grew from 100 000 to 1 400 000. This cut over one million from the jobless figures.

Germany was re-armed

New tanks, battleships, fighter planes and guns were built because Hitler was determined that Germany should become a great military power once more. Millions of jobs were created making these weapons and some businessmen made fortunes from huge government contracts.

The Nazis created jobs by sacking people

Many women and Jews lost their jobs when Hitler came to power. They were replaced by unemployed men.

FACT   *'I'm just putting my flour on!'*

Making weapons cost the Nazis a lot of money. To help pay for it, Hitler tried to make Germany **self-sufficient**. This meant replacing things bought from other countries with cheaper artificial substitutes made in Germany. For example, top German scientists found ways to make coffee from acorns, petrol from coal and make-up from flour.

▼ **Source C** *A German worker in 1985 describes why he supported Hitler in the 1930s.*

"I was unemployed for many years. I'd have made a deal with the devil to get work. Hitler came along and got me work so I followed him."

All workers had to join the **German Labour Front** run by Dr Robert Ley. This was a Nazi organisation that promised to protect the rights of workers and improve their conditions. No other trade unions were allowed.

The German Labour Front kept very strict control of workers. Everyone had to work and skilled men could be sent to do heavy labour like road building. Workers couldn't quit without the government's permission and their right to strike was removed. They could also be forced to work as many hours as the Nazis required. But not many workers complained. They may have been worried about the consequences of complaining but, by 1938, the average German was earning over ten times as much as he may have been receiving as dole money in 1932. Hitler had kept his promise to provide Germans with 'work and bread'.

WISE UP WORDS

- National Labour Service   conscription
  self-sufficient   German Labour Front

WORK

1 Look at **Source A**.
   a Who was this election poster aimed at?
   b How was it trying to appeal to them?
   c How successful do you think it would have been?

2 a Hitler once said, 'History will judge me according to whether I have succeeded in providing work.' What is *your* judgement? Copy and complete these statements for and against the argument that Hitler succeeded in providing work.

Yes, Hitler was successful	No, he wasn't successful
Before Hitler came to power, _____ Germans were unemployed. By 1939, only _____ had no job so Hitler created _____ jobs in six years.	Many of the jobs Hitler created were taken away from _____ and _____ so he didn't really create any new ones. Also, over _____ had to do military service so they didn't really have jobs, they were just training to fight. Men in the RAD weren't paid properly either, they just got _____, yet they were removed from the unemployment registers.

   b Write your own opinion. Was Hitler successful in providing work?

3 Why did the Nazis force all workers to join the German Labour Front?

3740 hours

Topic Focus

▸ To understand why Hitler rewarded people who worked hard.

Exam Focus

▸ To understand why the Nazis wanted to control people's leisure time, and how people were rewarded if they worked hard.

Hitler and the Nazis wanted to control every part of people's lives, even their spare or leisure time. They worked out that the average German spent between seven and eight hours a day sleeping and about six hours a day working. With typical Nazi efficiency, they calculated that ordinary Germans had about 10¼ hours a day free for leisure. This totalled 3740 hours a year. Hitler gave a doctor called Robert Ley the task of filling this spare time and making sure it wasn't wasted. So what did millions of ordinary Germans get up to when they weren't at work ... or in bed? And why were the Nazis so keen to control people's leisure time?

Hitler set up a special organisation called **Strength through Joy** (Kraft Durch Freude – KDF) to organise leisure activities for working people and to encourage hard work by providing rewards. Doctor Ley, the man in charge of the KDF, believed that people with nothing to do in their spare time might get angry and frustrated. They might even begin to think bad things about the Nazis and decide not to work very hard. Ley felt that workers with plenty to do in their spare time, and who were rewarded for their hard work, were more likely to do better at their jobs. So he organised a huge leisure programme of events and rewards aimed at filling as much of people's spare time as possible.

Two huge cruise ships were built that took workers on luxury holidays at bargain prices. Only the hardest workers were given places.

Skiing or walking holidays in the Alps. Travel, hotel and food cost about 25 marks – the equivalent of about one week's wages.

Three-week tours of Italy were offered (for the best workers) at a cost of 150 marks. Workers would stay in the best hotels and eat at the finest restaurants.

TOP EXAM TIP

The Nazis often talked about the creation of a national people's community. They called it their 'Volkgemeinschaft' and directed many policies towards creating their 'national identity'.

Over seven million people took part in sports matches organised by the KDF.

The KDF had its own band that toured all over Germany. Also, millions saw plays, musicals and operas for the first time – all organised by the KDF.

The KDF organised free evening classes for adults to learn new skills.

KRAFT DURCH FREUDE

▲ **Source A** *This photograph shows the 'People's Car' or* **Volkswagen**, *launched in 1938. Hitler said the car, designed by Ferdinand Porsche, 'should look like a beetle' because he admired the insect's tough, fighting nature. To help workers buy a car, the KDF started a savings scheme where workers paid five marks a week until 750 marks were in the bank. Then they received an order number entitling them to a car when it was made. Millions started to save for their 'Beetle' but the whole scheme was a swindle. Not one customer got their car – the money was used to build weapons instead!*

WISE UP WORDS

- Volkswagen   Strength through Joy

WORK

1. Imagine you work for Doctor Ley as a promotions expert in his Strength through Joy organisation. Draw a poster designed to promote the advantages of working hard in Nazi Germany. You want workers to see what rewards and benefits they could gain by putting in that extra bit of effort!

2. Look at **Source A**, including the label. Read this joke that went around Germany in 1939.

   'A car worker in the VW factory can't afford to buy his own car so smuggles parts and pieces out of the factory one by one, day by day. He takes them all home, hoping to put the car together when he has all the pieces. When the big day arrives, he puts it all together and makes a tank!'

   a. Explain what the joke means.

   b. What does this joke tell you about the attitude of some Germans to the Nazi government?

   c. What do you think would happen to you if you were reported to the police for telling the joke in 1939?

TOP EXAM TIP

Some historians have likened Hitler's approach to controlling Germany to a 'stick and carrot'. In other words, he introduced measures which were regarded as 'carrots' (to reward good people and attract them to the Nazi Party) and 'sticks' (to scare people into doing as they were told. Make sure you know examples of 'sticks' and 'carrots'.

What did you do at school today?

Topic Focus

▸ To understand the Nazi influence on schools and in lessons.

Exam Focus

▸ To be able to explain why the Nazis controlled schools and how they controlled them.

Hitler hoped to use the German school system to brainwash young Germans into loving him and the Nazi Party. He believed that children who learned to idolise him when they were young would continue to love him for the rest of their lives. He realised that in future he may have to call on these people to put up with hardships, to fight and perhaps even die for him. To get their undying loyalty, Hitler used every subject in school to put forward Nazi ideas and beliefs. He used education to produce 'ideal Nazis'. So what sort of things would you learn at school in Nazi Germany?

A young German schoolchild would have done a variety of subjects, including History, Geography, PE, Science and Maths. In History, students would learn about great German military victories and how badly Germany was treated at the end of the Great War. Geography lessons outlined areas of land in the world that Germany would soon conquer. Science lessons concentrated on weapon-making and chemical warfare whilst Maths lessons taught youngsters about bombing Jewish areas and asked them to calculate how much money Germany would save if they got rid of all disabled people (see **Source B**). The amount of time given over to PE trebled in the 1930s and a new subject, Race Studies or **Eugenics**, appeared on the timetable. Here, students were taught how to improve their race and about the Nazi belief in the inferiority of black people, eastern Europeans and, in particular, Jews. Textbooks were rewritten so that Nazi beliefs were taught as accepted facts and all teachers were made to put across Nazi ideas in their lessons.

Hitler even set up special academies known as the Adolf Hitler Schools or Order Castles, which took the very best students and tested them to their limits. After intense training, including many academic examinations and tough physical exercise, these youngsters graduated as 'ideal Nazis' – clever, tough and fiercely loyal to Hitler.

▸ **Source A** *A typical timetable for a day's education at a mixed school in Berlin, 1936. Boys and girls were* **indoctrinated** *slightly differently. Boys were taught to be the soldiers of the future, whilst the girls were prepared for lives as wives and mothers.*

	LESSON 1	LESSON 2	LESSON 3	DINNER	LESSON 4	LESSON 5	LESSON 6
BOYS	GERMAN	HISTORY/ GEOGRAPHY	EUGENICS/ NAZI THEORY	SPORT AND MUSIC CLUBS	PHYSICS AND CHEMISTRY	PE: BOXING, FOOTBALL AND MARCHING	MATHS
GIRLS	GERMAN	HISTORY/ GEOGRAPHY	EUGENICS/ NAZI THEORY		BIOLOGY/ HEALTH AND SEX EDUCATION	COOKERY	MATHS

▼ **Source B** *These questions have been translated and adapted from a German textbook during the Nazi period. All teachers had to join the German Nazi Teachers' League, which was set up to force teachers into teaching the Nazi message … or face the sack!*

"
Question 46: The Jews are aliens in Germany and shouldn't be here. In 1933, there were 66 060 000 people living in Germany. Of this total, 499 862 were Jews. What is the percentage of aliens in Germany?

Question 52: It costs, on average, four RM [Reichsmarks] a day to keep a cripple or a mentally ill person in hospital. There are currently 300 000 mental patients, lunatics and so on in Germany's hospitals. How much would the German nation save if they got rid of all these people?"

▼ **Source C** *A picture from a German school textbook entitled, 'Never trust a fox or a Jew'.*

▼ **Source D** *Part of a speech by Adolf Hitler, November 1933.*

"Your children are mine already. What are you? In time, you will die but your sons and daughters stand forever in my new Germany and in a short time, they'll know nothing else except this new Germany."

WISE UP WORDS

• indoctrinate   Eugenics

WORK

1 Look at **Source A**.
  a What is Eugenics?
  b Why do you think the Nazis insisted that all schoolchildren must be taught about Eugenics?
  c Why were boys and girls taught different things?
  d Look at your school timetable now. Suggest at least three ways the Nazis might change it.
    What subjects might they get rid of?
    What new subject might they introduce?
    What subjects might they change?

2 Look at **Source B**. Do you think the real aim of these questions was to improve children's maths skills?

3 Look at **Source C**.
  a Name the two racial groups of people shown in this source.
  b What do you think the Nazis wanted children who read this book to think? Explain your answer.

GCSE Question time
• What were the main features of the education of children in Nazi Germany?

Hitler Youth: are you tough enough?

Topic Focus

▸ To understand what Hitler's 'ideal' teenager was like, and how the Nazis trained them.

Exam Focus

▸ To be able to explain why millions of young Germans joined the Hitler Youth Organization, and explain the different ways boys and girls were trained.

In 1936, Hitler gave a speech that outlined what his ideal teenager should be like. He said that he wanted 'young men and women who can suffer pain ... they must be as fast as a greyhound, as tough as leather and as hard as steel'. So why did Hitler want young Germans to be so tough? What sort of things would young men and women be expected to do? And were young males and females trained in the same way?

Meet Peter Steiner, a 15-year-old member of the Hitler Youth Organisation. His sister, Elsbeth, is in a similar organisation for girls called the League of German Maidens. Read the information about Peter carefully – this is what life was like in Nazi Germany for nearly six million young people in 1936.

Peter joined a Nazi group called the 'Little Fellows' from age six to age ten. Then he joined the 'Young Folk' from 10 to 14. Finally, he became a fully-fledged member of the 'Hitler Youth' at 14. He will be part of the Hitler Youth until he is 18.

Peter attends a normal school but goes to Hitler Youth meetings several times a week after school. He attends special weekend camps every month.

At his Hitler Youth meetings, he learns how to march, fight with knives, fire a gun, play different sports and keep himself fit.

Achievement Award (see Source B)

Nazi Party armband

Hitler Youth Knife

strong hiking boots

He is a good cross-country runner and good at reading maps. He can hike 30 miles in one day.

The girls, who join the 'Young Girls' between 10 and 14 and the 'League of German Maidens' from 14 to 17, do not learn exactly the same as the boys. They still go on tough marches and attend weekend camps but they would mainly learn how to keep fit, cook good meals and look after babies. They are being prepared for motherhood.

Peter is encouraged to report his parents or teachers if they criticise Hitler or tell jokes about the Nazis.

▾ **Source A** *Having fun at a Hitler Youth camp in 1936. Note the tents in the background that all boys slept in.*

Leaders of Tomorrow

Kommende

▼ **Source B** *This series of tests is what a Hitler Youth boy, aged 10 to 14, would have been expected to do to get an 'Achievement Award'. Girls would do a similar series of tests but would be taught extra duties like learning to make a bed!*

To gain your Hitler Youth Achievement award:

1) Complete the following lessons:
   i)   Life of Hitler
   ii) Germans abroad
   iii) Germany's rightful place in the world
   iv) National holidays of the German people
   v) Five flag oaths
   vi) Six Hitler Youth songs

2) Complete the following athletic tests:
   i)   Run 60 metres in 10 seconds
   ii) Long jump 3.25 metres
   iii) Throw a small leather ball 35 metres
   iv) Pull up on a bar twice
   v) Somersault backwards twice
   vi) Swim 100 metres

3) Hiking and camping tests:
   i)   A day's hike of 15 kilometres
   ii) Camp in a tent for three days
   iii) Put up a two-man tent and take part in putting up a twelve-man tent
   iv) Make a cooking pit and find water for cooking
   v) Know the names of the most important trees
   vi) Use the stars to find your place on a map

4) Target practice:
   Hit a bull's eye on a target at a distance of eight metres with an air gun

▼ **Source C** *Membership of the Hitler Youth, 1933–1939. At first, membership of the Hitler Youth Organisation was not compulsory but the camps, sports activities and shooting practice proved too attractive for many youngsters. By 1936, Hitler had closed all other youth clubs and made membership of the Hitler Youth compulsory, although some still refused to join (see fact box). However, by 1939, the vast majority of young Germans were part of the Hitler Youth.*

Year	Membership	Population of Germany aged 10–18
1933	2 292 041	7 529 000
1934	3 577 565	7 682 000
1935	3 943 033	8 172 000
1936	5 437 601	8 656 000
1937	5 879 955	9 060 000
1938	7 031 266	9 109 000
1939	7 287 470	8 870 000

FACT *Did all young people support the Nazis?*

Not all young Germans liked what they saw of the Nazi way of life. Richer youngsters who refused to join the Hitler Youth went to parties, listened to American jazz music (banned by the Nazis because of its black origins) and had Jewish friends. They were known as **Swing types**. Other working-class youngsters formed gangs – 'The Roving Dudes', 'The **Edelweiss Pirates**', 'The Navajos' – which went camping and sang songs which made fun of Hitler. They even physically attacked Hitler Youth groups. These gangs included boys *and* girls, including Jews.

WISE UP WORDS

- Edelweiss Pirates   Swing types

WORK

1 **a** Using the information and evidence on these two pages, write two diary entries for a weekend away at a Hitler Youth camp. You could include details about:
- the skills you are learning and activities you are taking part in;
- your uniform;
- your reasons for joining the Hitler Youth Organisation;
- the famous Achievement Award (see **Source B** – the examination for this would take place on the camps!);
- any youngster you know who <u>hasn't</u> joined the Hitler Youth. Do you know why? What do they do in their spare time?

Note: if you are writing as a boy, you might make a note of what the girls are doing and vice versa. You might even write *why* boys and girls train differently.

   b Why do you think Hitler and the Nazis put so much effort into organising the lives of young people?

2 Look at **Source C**. Why do you think the Nazi Youth Organisation attracted so many youngsters?

'Set the husband free'

Topic Focus

▶ To understand how women lost out under Nazi rule, and how Nazis attempted to reward 'productive' women.

Exam Focus

▶ How did the Nazis change the lives of women in Germany?

Read **Source A** carefully. This is an amazing – and shocking – Nazi idea from 1943 that never quite became a law. Despite not coming into effect, it still shows us exactly what Hitler and the Nazis thought about women: their job was to have as many children as possible … and if they already had lots of children, they should 'set their husband free' to go and get other women pregnant!

The Nazis had strong views about the role of women in German society. They felt it was their patriotic duty to stay at home, have lots of children and support their husbands. Hitler even summed up their role for them when he said they should stick to the **three Ks** – Kinder, Kirche and Küche or children, church and cooking. From the start, women were not equal. Within months of Hitler coming to power, many female doctors, teachers, lawyers and judges were sacked. Getting qualifications and a professional job was discouraged as it might get in the way of producing children. Women were even banned from jury service because the Nazis said they were unable to think without emotion!

▼ **Source A**

> "All single and married women up to the age of 35, who do not already have four children, <u>must</u> have four children. The fathers should be racially pure German men. It does not matter if these men are married or not. Any family that already has four children must set the husband free for this action."

The Nazis tried to interfere in other aspects of women's lives. In many cities, women were banned from smoking because it was 'unladylike'. Wearing make-up, trousers, high heels or dyeing hair was also discouraged for the same reason. In fact, the only thing that women were actively encouraged to do was to have children. Loans were given out to newly married couples – the equivalent of a year's wages – to encourage them to have children.

◀ **Source B** A Nazi poster of 1937 showing what the Nazis thought a woman's role in life should be. Look for: i) the plain, simple image of a woman breastfeeding her baby. Note that her hair is in a very simple style; ii) her husband working on the land, providing for Germany whilst his wife takes care of things at home; iii) the church in the background, another one of Hitler's 'three Ks'.

On the birth of a first child, they could keep a quarter of the money. On the birth of another, they could keep the second quarter. They could keep the third quarter on the birth of a third child and then keep the lot on the birth of a fourth.

The Nazis banned contraception and abortion too. Even slimming was discouraged because being slim was not thought to be good for getting pregnant. Every year, on 12 August, the birthday of Hitler's mother, the Motherhood Medal was awarded to women who had the most children. Mothers with eight children received the 'Gold Cross'.

▼ **Source C** *Comments made by Nazi leaders about the role of women in German society.*

- The woman belongs to the smaller world – her husband, her family, her children and her home.

- Women have their battlefield too: with each child she brings into the world for the nation, she is fighting her fight on behalf of the nation.

- Women have the task of being beautiful and bringing children into the world.

▼ **Source D** *This flag was displayed above homes known as **Lebensborn** – the Spring of Life. Some called them maternity homes – others called them brothels! Unmarried women could visit and stay there with the aim of becoming pregnant by one of Hitler's 'racially pure' SS soldiers.*

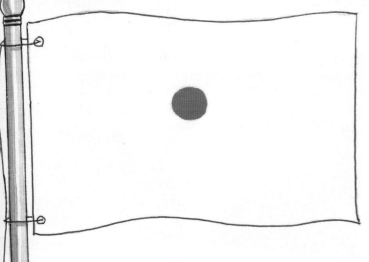

▼ **Source E** *An advertisement in a German newspaper, 1936.*

52-year-old doctor. Fought in Great War. Wishes to settle down. Wants a male child through marriage to a young, healthy, virgin, Aryan woman. She should be undemanding, used to heavy work, not a spender, with flat heels, without earrings, if possible without money.

WISE UP WORDS
- Lebensborn   three Ks

WORK

1 Look at **Source A**. Explain how this law was designed to encourage couples to have large families.

2 Look at **Source B**. How useful is this source as evidence of the role of women in Nazi Germany?

3 Look at **Source E**.

   a Describe in your own words the kind of woman this doctor wanted to marry.

   b Why do you think the doctor wanted to get married?

   c Can you think of a reason why the doctor would prefer a woman 'without money'?

   d Do you think the Nazis would approve or disapprove of this advert? Give reasons for your answer.

   e Do you think you would be allowed to place this advert in a newspaper today? Explain your answer.

4 In a small group (or on your own if you prefer), design and produce a leaflet or booklet that aims to promote: i) the ideal German woman; ii) large families.

   You might want to present it like a guidebook with 'top tips', an interesting title, drawings and information. Why not include a message from the Führer himself?

The Olympic Games, 1936: success or failure?

Topic Focus

▶ These pages will help you to understand why the Nazis tried to turn the 1936 Olympics into one of the greatest shows on earth.

Exam Focus

▶ Was the 1936 Olympic Games a complete success for Nazi Germany and the 'Master Race'?

The Olympic Games is one of the most exciting and popular sporting events in the world. In 1936, they were held in Berlin, Germany, and Hitler decided to deliberately use the Games to show the world how splendid Nazi Germany was. He also thought they could be used as a showcase for his belief that his German master race was fitter, faster and stronger than all other races. So were the Berlin Olympics of 1936 a Nazi success story? Did the Olympics show the world how wonderful the Nazis were? Did everything go exactly to plan?

The Germans built a brand new stadium to host most of the action. It held 100 000 people and used the most advanced lighting system and most sophisticated 'photo finish' equipment ever made. The stadium had the largest stop clock ever built and TV cameras were used to record all the action for the first time.

▼ **Source A** *From a textbook written by a modern historian. Joseph Goebbels was put in charge of the Games by Hitler himself.*

"With guests and competitors from 49 countries coming in to the heart of Nazi Germany, it was going to take all Goebbels' talents to show that Germany was a modern, civilised and successful nation. No expense was spared. When the Games opened, the visitors were duly amazed at the scale of the stadium, the wonderful facilities and the efficiency of the organisation. However, they were also struck by, and in some cases appalled by, the almost fanatical devotion of the people to Hitler and the ... presence of ... soldiers who were standing guard everywhere."

▼ **Source B** *From an American book written about Nazi Germany in 1959. Some countries considered pulling out of the Games because of reports about the way the Nazis treated German Jews. In response, the Nazis included one token Jew in their Olympic squad.*

"The signs saying 'Jews not welcome' were quietly taken down from shops and hotels, the persecution of the Jews halted for a time and the country put on its best behaviour."

▼ **Source C** *The brand new state-of-the-art Olympic stadium complex. This aerial photograph shows a capacity crowd viewing both athletics and swimming.*

To Hitler's great joy, the German Olympic squad performed much better than anyone expected. They won more medals than any other country – 33 gold, 26 silver and 30 bronze. This, Hitler claimed, showed how talented and strong the Aryan race was and how it was superior to all others.

However, to Hitler's annoyance, a black American athlete named Jesse Owens became the star of the Games. He won four gold medals (100 and 200 metre sprints, long jump and 4 X 100 metre relay), breaking 11 world records on the way. So much for Nazi beliefs about white, Aryan Germans being fitter, faster and stronger than all others! Not surprisingly, Hitler refused to present Owens with his medals or shake the hand of the man who single-handedly showed Hitler's racial theories to be nonsense.

▼ **Source D** *Jesse Owens, the black American athlete and winner of four Olympic gold medals, being photographed in August 1936.*

▼ **Source E** *Hitler's view on race, as reported by Albert Speer, a leading Nazi.*

"Hitler was annoyed by the successes of Jesse Owens. He said that such people had an unfair advantage over civilised white people because they were descended from jungle primitives. They were unfair competition and would be excluded from future games."

WORK

1 Why were the Nazis so keen to host the 1936 Olympic Games?

2 Look at **Source A**.
  a According to this source, what impressed many of the visitors?
  b Why were some 'appalled'?

3 Look at **Source B**.
  a Why do you think the persecution of the Jews was 'halted for a time' during the Games?
  b Why do you think the Germans included one Jew in their Olympic squad?

4 Look at **Sources D** and **E**. Why did the performance of Jesse Owens matter so much to Hitler?

5 In your opinion, were the 1936 Olympic Games a Nazi success story or not? When answering, you may consider whether the Games showed that:
  i) Nazi Germany was a modern, hi-tech country;
  ii) Nazi Germany was well organised and disciplined;
  iii) Aryan Germans were superior to all others.

TOP EXAM TIP

The Berlin Olympics can be viewed as both a success AND a failure for the Nazis. Know why you might view it as both a success and a failure.

Why did Kristallnacht take place?

Topic Focus

▶ These four pages will help you to form an opinion on why so much Jewish property was destroyed in November 1938, and who was responsible for the destruction.

Exam Focus

▶ To understand what took place on Kristallnacht and the way ordinary Germans felt about it.

Early in November 1938, a German man working for the German government in Paris was shot dead by a Jew. The Jew claimed he was seeking revenge for the bad treatment his parents had received by the Nazis. On 9 November, Jewish homes, shops and **synagogues** were attacked all over Germany. Ninety-one Jews were murdered and over 20 000 were arrested and taken to concentration camps. Most were later released only when they promised to leave Germany for good. These events were called **Kristallnacht** (Crystal Night) because of all the glass that was broken.

The Nazis claimed that the events of Kristallnacht were carried out by ordinary Germans who were fed up with Jews in Germany. Some thought it was ordered by Hitler himself. Another theory is that it was planned by Goebbels – a leading Nazi and personal friend of Hitler – in an attempt to please his Führer.

What do *you* think? How will *you* interpret the evidence? Why do *you* think Kristallnacht took place? Study all the sources carefully before arriving at your conclusion.

▼ **Source A** *A headline from a German newspaper, 10 November. Note: all newspapers were either owned by the Nazi Party or were supporters of them.*

Jewish homes attacked

Spontaneous waves of anger amongst the German people sweep nation as a result of the cowardly murder of German in Paris

▼ **Source B** *A description of events in the weeks before Kristallnacht, written in November 1938 by a German Jew. Does this source support the evidence of **Source A** about Kristallnacht?*

"There had been signs of trouble for weeks. Notices reading 'Jews not wanted' appeared in various shops and cinemas. In the countryside, Jews were terrorised so much that they sold their belongings and moved away."

▼ **Source C** *Comments by German men and women about Kristallnacht, reported in* Hitler's Germany *by Bernt Engelmann, 1988.*

"An hour later I took the bus into town... Everywhere I went I saw upset, sad or angry faces. I also heard three people's comments:

- 'Once upon a time looters and robbers were shot, now the police protect them. That's what Germany's come to. The country we risked our lives for'. **An old soldier watching people steal from shops with shattered windows.**

- 'They shouldn't have done it. I'm sure Hitler doesn't approve.' **A woman wearing a large Nazi Party badge.**

- 'We Germans will pay dearly for what was done last night. Our churches, houses and stores will be destroyed for sure.' **An older German woman.**

▼ **Source D** *A historian's summary of a journalist's account of a dinner on the evening of 9 November. The journalist wrote his account in 1954.*

"The Nazi leaders were having dinner in Munich on 9 November when an officer came in and whispered something to Goebbels, who turned and muttered to Hitler. Goebbels could be heard explaining about an attack he was going to launch in a few hours time. Hitler approved because he squealed with delight and slapped his thigh with enthusiasm. It was clear that Goebbels, who was not popular with Hitler at the time, was trying to win back Hitler's support."

▼ **Source E** *Adapted extract from a book written in 1978 by David Irving called* The War Path. *Note how the content of this source differs from* **Source D**. *Can you think of reasons why these interpretations differ?*

"Goebbels was at Hitler's home when word arrived of the death in Paris. He told Hitler that there had been demonstrations against Jews in two German cities.

Hitler said that the Nazi Party were not to organise such demonstrations — nor stop them if they just happened. (Note: this is what Goebbels said at the secret enquiry set up by the Nazi Party after the attacks.) Goebbels then left to speak at a meeting … he told the meeting that more demonstrations were to be organised by the Nazi Party but they must not appear to be behind it. These instructions were put out to local Nazis throughout Germany … an orgy of burning and destruction, murder and rape began. Hitler rang Goebbels at 1:00am to ask, 'What's the game?' and at 2:56am, a message was sent out to stop the attacks."

▼ **Source F** *An anonymous letter sent to a British official working in Germany from a man who worked for the German government, 12 November 1938.*

"I feel the urge to present to you a true report of the recent riots, plundering and destruction of Jewish property. Despite what the Nazis say, the German people have nothing to do with these riots and burnings. The police supplied SA men [Hitler's brownshirted private army] with axes, house-breaking tools and ladders. A list of the addresses of all Jewish shops and flats was provided and the mob set to work. The police had strict orders not to interfere."

▼ **Source G** *Albert Speer, a man who worked as Hitler's chief architect, remembering Kristallnacht. After the war, Speer spent 20 years in prison for his work in Nazi Germany.*

"On 10 November I drove past the still smouldering ruins of Berlin's synagogues … today this memory is one of the saddest of my life. Hitler claimed he had not wanted this. Later, in private, Goebbels hinted that he had been the organiser for this sad and terrible night and I think it very possible that he was."

▼ **Source H** *An interpretation of a cartoon about Kristallnacht published in a British magazine on 30 November 1938. The woman represents the German people. The man in uniform is a Nazi.*

▼ **Source I** *Total property destroyed. From a report written by one leading Nazi (Heydrich) to another (Goering).*

Synagogues	191 destroyed 76 completely demolished
Jews	20 000 arrested
Foreigners	Three arrested
Looting	There has been looting of Jewish shops and warehouses 174 people have been arrested
Businesses	815 have been destroyed

WISE UP WORDS

• synagogues looting Kristallnacht

WORK

Your task is to establish why Kristallnacht took place. To do this effectively, you will have to analyse the evidence on these four pages very carefully.

1 Copy out and complete the chart below. Analysis of the first source has been started for you, although there are other things you could say about **Source A**. Complete for all the sources.

Source	What is it?	What does it say about the cause of Kristallnacht?	Is the source reliable?
A	News report from a German newspaper in 1938.	That the German people were responsible and acted as a result of the murder of a German in Paris.	Not really, the Nazis owned the newspapers and would decide the way in which news was presented...

2 Now read the following two statements. Each opinion has been given as a reason why Kristallnacht took place. Write down which one you agree with, giving reasons for your choice based on the evidence.

Statement 1: 'Kristallnacht happened as a result of a well-organised Nazi campaign that used the assassination of a German in Paris as an excuse. Most ordinary Germans were not involved in the events.'

Statement 2: 'Kristallnacht happened in a Germany that hated Jews and was ready to attack and rob them at a moment's notice. When ordinary Germans heard of the killing of a German in Paris, they took to the streets to seek their revenge.'

Hitler's henchmen

Topic Focus

▸ To understand how Hitler spent his days, and who the people were who helped him to run Germany.

Exam Focus

▸ Describe at least two of Hitler's 'henchmen' and explain their roles within Nazi Germany.

Hitler didn't run Germany on his own. He needed help – lots of it. In fact, most historians now agree that Hitler didn't work very hard at all. He would sleep until late in the morning, have a long lunch, go for a walk, watch films and read books before having dinner and going to bed late. Important decisions were made only occasionally, usually during long chats with leading members of the Nazi Party. It was then up to these people to go away and carry out 'the will of the Führer' as they called it.

Hitler's followers – known as 'henchmen' – were the ones who really controlled Nazi Germany. So who were the most important of Hitler's helpers?

Hermann Goering (1893–1946)

- From a very rich family.
- Fighter pilot in World War One, awarded medals for bravery.
- Joined Nazi Party in 1922, wounded in Munich Putsch of 1923.
- Built up German air force and was later responsible for preparing Germany for war – his Four Year Plans built up weapons and tried to increase coal, oil and rubber production in Germany so they didn't have to go to other countries to buy goods.
- Some said he was fat, big-headed, childish, greedy and a drug addict.
- Committed suicide (poison) in 1946 whilst on trial at the end of the war.

Goering is pictured here in one of his favourite uniforms. This wasn't an official Nazi colour; Goering just liked it so chose it for his own uniform! Goebbels once described him as having the heart of a child – indeed, he loved playing with his train set and dressing up in strange costumes.

Joseph Goebbels (1897–1945)

- Son of a poor manual worker.

- Couldn't fight in World War One because of a disability in his leg.

- Joined Nazi Party in 1922. Didn't like Hitler at first but soon grew to admire him.

- In charge of Nazi propaganda – he was intelligent, well educated and a brilliant speaker. In 1943, he was also put in charge of defending Germany and organising civilians during World War Two.

- Poisoned his six children and his wife before shooting himself in 1945, shortly before the end of the war.

Goebbels is pictured here with his daughter Helga, on holiday in 1935. He would eventually kill all his children!

Heinrich Himmler (1900–1945)

- Son of a teacher. Failed to make a living as a chicken farmer.

- Joined German army in 1918 but didn't fight in World War One.

- Joined Nazi Party in 1923, took part in Munich Putsch.

- In charge of the SS, Gestapo and all concentration camps.

- From 1941, he took charge of the 'Final Solution' – the mass murder of all Europe's Jews.

- Timid, clumsy, fainted at the sight of Jews being killed.

- Committed suicide in 1945 soon after capture by American soldiers.

Himmler is pictured here in full SS uniform. Note the skull and crossbones cap badge – the sign of the dreaded Death's Head Unit of the SS, the group in charge of all concentration and death camps.

FACT *Any henchwomen?*

As you might expect, the top Nazi jobs were taken by men. The highest ranking female member of the Nazi government was Gertrude Scholz Klink, the head of the Nazi Women's Bureau. She was tall, blonde, racially pure, had four children and loved the Nazis. However, even she complained that she was completely ignored at important meetings!

Martin Bormann (1900–?)

- Son of a postman, fought briefly in World War One.

- Joined the Nazi Party in 1925. Worked hard to raise money for the Nazis.

- Very powerful. Was in charge of **Gauleiters** (Nazi area leaders) so knew exactly what orders were given and who was doing what. Kept secret files on all leading Nazis, including Hitler!

- Worked as Hitler's secretary, his second-in-command and his personal bodyguard. Had control over anyone who wanted to see Hitler.

- Ambitious, clever, cold and calculating – Hitler trusted him completely.

- Disappeared without trace on 1 May 1945. Did he survive the war and live out the rest of his life secretly in South America?

Bormann, photographed in 1939. In the last years of Nazi rule, no one other than Hitler was more powerful in Germany. He is the least well known of Hitler's 'inner circle' and is sometimes called the 'forgotten Nazi'!

Reinhard Heydrich (1904–1942)

- Son of a musician, well educated. Had a Jewish grandfather!

- After a brief spell in the navy, he joined the Nazi Party in 1931.

- Officially in charge of the Gestapo from 1936 (so was Himmler's deputy) and responsible for controlling Czechoslovakia after the German invasion. Also in charge of the murder of physically and mentally disabled people who Nazis no longer wanted.

- Like Himmler, he played a key role in the extermination of Jews. During the war, he was in personal control of murder squads that patrolled the countryside looking for Jews to kill.

- Some said he was ruthless, selfish, calculating and evil. Had ambitions to become leader of Germany.

- Assassinated in Prague in 1942 by British-trained Czech freedom fighters. In response to his death, the Nazis burned whole villages and killed at least 10 000 people.

Heydrich, pictured in 1940. One historian described him as the 'demonic master of evil ... the high priest of Nazi racism'. His nicknames included 'the Blond Beast', 'the Hangman' and 'the Butcher'.

FACT *Who did what?*

Leading Nazis competed with each other to come up with new ideas or outrageous plans to please their Führer ... and this is exactly how Hitler liked it. He enjoyed playing people off against each other – to 'divide and rule' as some called it – in order to make his own position as leader even more secure.

WISE UP WORD

- Gauleiters

WORK

1 a Describe a typical day in the life of Adolf Hitler.

   b Do you think most ordinary Germans knew how Hitler spent his time? Explain your answer.

   c How were important decisions made in Nazi Germany?

2 a Copy and complete the chart.

Henchman	Family background	Early life	Work for the Nazis	Character	Death

   b Imagine you work for a publishing company which is about to release a book called *Hitler's Henchmen*. Your boss wants to put a picture of one of the famous henchmen on the cover and has asked you to pick one. But whose picture will you choose? Will your choice be based on who had the most power, who was the most famous or who was the closest to Hitler? Will you pick the most ruthless or the hardest worker?

   Write a 100-word proposal explaining your choice to your boss.

   c Why don't you think any women ever got any of the really important jobs in Nazi Germany?

Have you been learning?

TASK 1 Word hunt

Draw this puzzle into your book and fill in the answers to the clues. A word will reveal itself in the middle (*clue 11*). Write a sentence or two about how the Nazis used this mystery word.

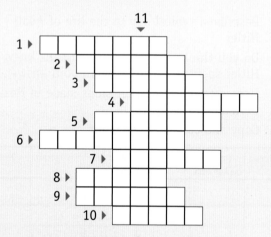

Clue 1　Secret police

Clue 2　Supreme leader

Clue 3　'Night of the _____ Glass'

Clue 4　Designer of the 'People's Car'

Clue 5　'Schutz _____' – full name of the dreaded SS

Clue 6　'_____ through Joy' – organised leisure time

Clue 7　National _____ Service – all 18- to 25-year-olds joined for six months

Clue 8　Last name of the 1936 Olympic sprint hero

Clue 9　First of the 'three Ks'

Clue 10　A huge Nazi meeting with speeches, parades, fireworks and music

TASK 2 Prejudice

The word 'bias' means one-sided. There is a lot of bias in history where only one side of the picture is shown. Perhaps only the good points – or the bad points – of something are presented, but never both. Bias exaggerates or distorts what has been said or done. An advertisement on the TV is an example of bias. It doesn't ever tell you the bad points of the product … or that you may be able to buy better, cheaper versions from somewhere else!

'Prejudice' is an extreme form of bias – where an artist or a writer, for example, reveals their dislike or hatred for a particular person, race, minority group, class of people or way of life. In Nazi Germany, prejudice was everywhere!

Study this picture carefully. It appeared in a German school textbook in the 1930s. Then answer the questions at the top of the next page.

a How have the Jewish children and the adult on the left been drawn? Describe your feelings as you look at them.

b What is one of the Jewish children doing to the schoolgirl on the right? What does this make you feel about Jewish children?

c How are the non-Jewish children drawn?

d How do the non-Jewish children react to the departure of the Jews?

e The Nazis controlled all pictures that appeared in school textbooks. What does this picture tell us about the Nazis?

f Why do you think the Nazis targeted children with their prejudiced pictures?

TASK 3 Question time

Look at these genuine GCSE questions carefully. Why not try to complete one, two or even all of them as a revision exercise? In brackets after each question, you will find the pages of this book where there is information that might refresh your memory.

- 'Propaganda was the main way in which the Nazis controlled the German people.' Do you agree with this statement? Explain your answer. (pages 46–47)

- Why was opposition to the Nazis so weak? (pages 44–47)

- Explain why Hitler set up the Nazi Youth movements. (pages 62–63)

- Why were women and children such an important part of Hitler's plans for Germany? (pages 64–65)

- The following were factors that enabled the Nazis to influence young people in Germany:

  i) Nazi education policy;

  ii) Nazi youth organisations;

  iii) persecution.

  Which of these factors do you think was *most* important? Explain your answer, referring to i, ii and iii. (pages 60–63)

- How much did people benefit from Nazi rule? Explain your answer. (pages 56–59)

TASK 4 'I talked to Hitler'

The following source is based on a news story that appeared in the *Daily Express* in November 1936. It was written by David Lloyd George, a respected and popular politician, who had been Britain's Prime Minister between 1916 and 1922.

Read the source carefully and answer the questions that follow:

Daily Express

'I talked to Hitler' by David Lloyd George

I have just returned from a visit to Germany. I have now seen the famous German leader and something of the great changes he has made. Whatever you may think of his methods – and they are certainly not those of a parliamentary country – there can be no doubt that he has achieved a marvellous transformation in the spirit of the people, in their attitude to each other and in their outlook. One man has accomplished this miracle. He is a born leader of men – a national leader.

a In your own words, explain how you think David Lloyd George felt about Hitler.

b List the things that David Lloyd George might have been shown on his visit to Germany that made him believe that a 'marvellous transformation' had taken place.

c What things in Germany do you think David Lloyd George wasn't shown on his visit?

d What do you think David Lloyd George meant when he wrote that Hitler's methods of ruling Germany were 'certainly not those of a parliamentary country'?

A Simple Guide To Mind Mapping

So what's a mind map?

Mind mapping is a special way of taking notes. Mind maps use only key words, phrases and images. They are quick to make, and because they look so interesting, many people find the information contained in them much easier to remember than other ways of making notes.

Why mind maps work

Mind maps helps you to quickly identify and understand the way pieces of the information fit together to build up the 'big picture'. They can help you revise all sorts of things, from detailed exam questions to whole topics.

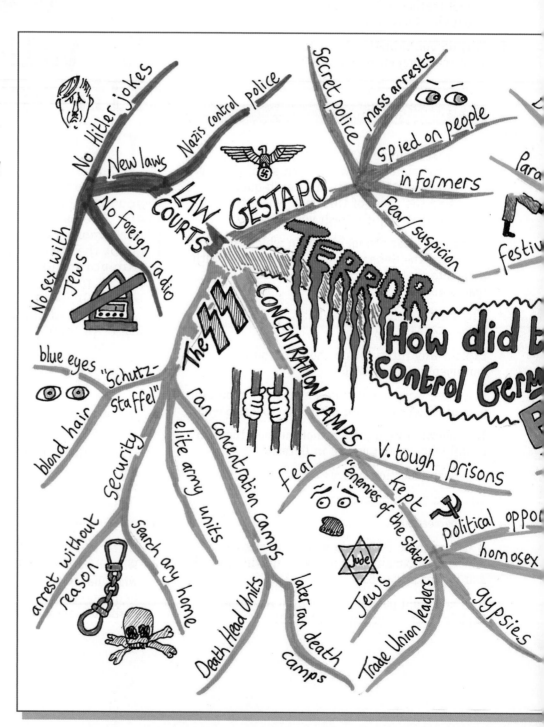

How to mind map

- Take a large sheet of paper and turn it to landscape.
- Write the topic/problem/question in the middle of the sheet and draw a frame around it. If you can make the centre a clear, strong visual image that fits in with the general theme of the mind map. When mind mapping anything on the Nazis, for example, the swastika is the perfect example to include instead of 'Nazi Party'.

- 'Branch Out' from the centre with the main ideas (like the branches of a tree) that you think about when looking at the central theme. Keep branching with each new 'association'.
- Put keywords on the lines – this helps reinforce your notes.
- Print, rather than write in your usual 'joined up' writing. This makes it easier to read and remember. Some people think lower case is easier to remember than upper case too! So avoid doing your whole mind map in capital letters.
- Use **colour** to make things stand out. Things that stand out on the page will stand out in your mind.
- Use arrows, images and small (even silly) pictures wherever possible.
- Put down ideas as soon as they enter your mind – don't hold back. If you dry up in one area, move on to another branch – and if you run out of space, don't start a new sheet, just stick some paper on the side.
- Tony Buzan, one of the inventors of mind mapping, on www.mind-mapping.co.uk says: 'Have fun! Add a little humour, exaggeration or absurdity wherever you can. Your brain will delight in getting the maximum use and enjoyment from this process and will therefore learn faster, recall more effectively and think more clearly.'

Mind maps help you to break away from the 'normal' way or revising, which often consists of making long lists of facts. They are more compact than the typical way of making notes often taking up just one side of paper. And the way you complete them engages the creative part of your brain, helping you to write more freely and opening you up to new ways of thinking. Their colourful, interesting shape and structure stimulates your brain in to helping you to remember the information within it.

DO IT YOURSELF: Why not try mind mapping topics such as 'Germany and the Great War', 'Adolf Hitler 1889-1919' or 'The Streseman Years' as well as real GCSE questions such as 'How did Hitler become Chancellor in 1933?' or 'What was the Hitler Youth Movement?'.

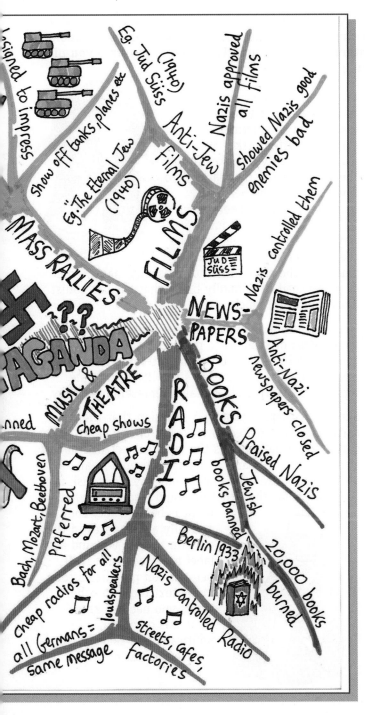

How to Analyse Cartoons

You will come across all sorts of evidence in your history studies – drawings, paintings, diaries, posters, speeches, photographs and news articles. But one of the most common sources to appear in textbooks and on exam papers are political cartoons and understanding them properly should really help you pick up extra marks in your exams!

You will come across all sorts of evidence in your history studies – drawings, paintings, diaries, posters, speeches, photographs and news articles. But one of the most common sources to appear in textbooks and on exam papers are political cartoons and understanding them properly should really help you pick up extra marks in your exams!

So What are Political Cartoons?

When we talk about 'cartoons' in relation to your History studies, we are not talking about Scooby Doo or Donald Duck! The type of cartoons used time and time again in history lessons, textbooks and

exam papers are 'political cartoons', the sort that have appeared in newspapers for many years.

Like photographs, newspaper articles, diaries, speeches, paintings and political documents, a cartoon is a key historical source. And correctly interpreting the message of a political cartoon can help us understand important events, people and even opinions at the time the cartoon was created.

What Makes a Political Cartoon?

Understanding cartoons correctly can be very tough! There are however several basic elements to look out for...

Firstly, there is usually a caricature or a key individual featured in the picture. The cartoonist often makes the person look silly or pokes fun at them. One of the first tasks is to work out who the person is. Does the way have been drawn tell you something about the way the cartoonist feels about them? After all, if the main

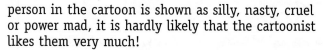

person in the cartoon is shown as silly, nasty, cruel or power mad, it is hardly likely that the cartoonist likes them very much!

In cartoons you may also come across national stereotypes or symbols to represent a particular country. John Bull or Britannia often represent Britain; Uncle Sam represents the USA, Marianne represents France and Germania represents Germany.

Secondly, there is usually a situation that the cartoonist has created to make his or her point. The cartoonist usually places the main subject within this situation or scene and exaggerates events in an attempt to make us feel a certain way. Your task is to work out what the situation could mean and what

point is being made. Look carefully at the dates in the cartoon to help you and any label that goes with it. It helps if you put the cartoon in context too – in other words you need to know what was going on, politically and socially, at the time it was drawn.

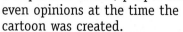

Top Tips

There are a number of key processes to go through when analysing cartoons.

Look at the background – what impression does it give? War clouds often appear in the run up to major conflicts for example.

Think about the cartoonist – where is he or she from? What do you think they think about the events they have drawn? Can you detect whether they are being supportive of events or of the main person in the cartoon ... or are they criticising them? Think about the point the cartoonist is trying to make.

ANALYSING CARTOONS

Look at the things the cartoonist has drawn – what or who has been drawn and how have they been drawn? Make a list if you need to.

Date the cartoon – what was happening at the time and who was involved in the events?

Put it into Practice

The following source is a classic political cartoon from the 1930s. It appeared in a British newspaper in July 1936 just after 'The Night of the Long Knives' (see pg. 37 for more detail) had taken place. Work through the analysis carefully.

Pause for thought: The cartoon below is a good example of where a student needs to know about the events of the time. Nowhere on the cartoon does it mention 'The Night of the Long Knives' – the examiner assumes you know all about this event.

The SA (Brownshirts) were formed in 1921. Made up mainly of ex-soldiers, they were Hitler's private army of Nazi thugs who protected his meetings and beat up opponents in the early years. By the time Hitler became Germany's leader, they were a bit of an embarrassment for him. He was safely in power and didn't need these bullies

Joseph Goebbels was one of Hitler's most loyal Nazis. Why do you think he's been drawn in this way?

Army leaders hated the SA, calling them 'thieves, drunks and sods', but Hitler needed the army on his side, they had an important role to play in Germany's future!

Herman Goering was a fierce Nazi who was a very patriotic German. Here he is shown as a Viking. Note the spear dripping with blood.

The title of the poster, what point do you think is being made with this phrase?

How has the cartoonist drawn Hitler? Do you think he supports Hitler's actions? The cartoonist has called the Swastika on Hitler's sleeve surrounded by the words "The Double Cross". Why do you think he uses this term? It is important to remember here that the SA had done a lot for Hitler in the early years, and now was attacking them. Also, note the 'smoking gun'. Why has this been drawn?

Hitler used the powerful SA (Brownshirts or Stormtroopers) as a threat. There were four million of them – and they were loyal not only to Hitler, but to their SA leader, Ernst Roehm. On the night of the 30th June 1934 hundreds of key leaders in the SA were arrested and shot. It became known as 'The Night of the Long Knives' ... and any threat from the SA was now over!

Hitler goes to war

Topic Focus

➤ To understand how Hitler intended to make Germany a powerful nation once more, after it suffered defeat at the end of World War One.

Exam Focus

➤ How was Germany punished at the end of the World War One, and what did Hitler intend to do to restore Germany's power?

One of Hitler's main aims was to make Germany a powerful nation once more. He had fought as a losing soldier in the Great War of 1914–1918 and, like millions of Germans, was humiliated by the punishment Germany received at the end of the fighting (see **Source A**).

▼ **Source A** *A summary of the Treaty of Versailles – the agreement reached at the end of the Great War. No German representatives were allowed to discuss the treaty – they just had to accept it – or face invasion. Not surprisingly, the German people hated it. Hitler swore revenge!*

Treaty of Versailles

• The Great War is Germany's fault so they must pay for it. The money will go to the winning countries. They are to pay £6 600 000 000 (in instalments up to 1988!)

• Germany must be made weak. They are allowed only a small army (100 000 men), a small navy (six battleships) and no submarines, fighter planes or tanks.

• Germany must hand over some of its land (about 10% in total) to the winning countries. They will lose 16% of their coalfields and half their iron and steel industries. Some of the land will be used to make new countries like Czechoslovakia and Poland.

• Germany must never unite with Austria ever again.

• No German soldiers can go in the Rhineland, an area of Germany which borders France.

Signed: Britain, France, USA, Italy and other winning countries

Hitler identified three things that he felt he must do in order to make Germany a world power once more:

i) he wanted to get all the land back that Germany lost after the Great War. He felt he had to build up his army, navy and air force to do this;

ii) he wanted to join together all German-speaking people into one big country;

iii) he wanted to make Germany even bigger because he believed that true Germans were such a great and powerful race that they needed the extra living space (he called it **Lebensraum**) to reach their full potential. He realised that he may have to take land from smaller, weaker countries in order to do this.

Hitler knew that it would mean breaking the Treaty of Versailles if he were to achieve his three main objectives … but he didn't care! Hitler, like millions of Germans, hated the treaty and would carry on with his master plan regardless (see **Source B**).

▼ **Source B** *A speech by Adolf Hitler.*

"The Treaty of Versailles is engraved on the minds and hearts of the German people. It is burned into them. Sixty million people find their souls aflame with a feeling of rage and shame. The people are joined in a common cry: 'We will have weapons again'."

Three days after becoming leader of Germany, Hitler ordered his military chiefs to start secretly building new tanks, submarines, battleships and fighter planes. This was known as **rearmament**. He ordered that every young man had to have army training in the new, bigger, German army. This was known as conscription. Then he took Germany out of the League of Nations, an international peacekeeping organisation set up after the Great War. The chances of a peaceful future didn't look good!

▼ ***Source C*** *Hitler checks out some of his new troops in 1936. The style of marching shown in the photograph is known as 'goose-stepping'.*

In late 1935, Hitler told the world about his increased army, navy and air force ... but no one did anything! Some countries didn't want to stand up to Hitler because they were scared Germany might invade, whilst others felt that Germany should be allowed to build up their armed forces if they wanted to. After all, they were only protecting themselves, weren't they?

In 1936, Hitler got more daring. He sent German soldiers into the Rhineland, an area of Germany next to France where German soldiers were forbidden to go (see **Source A**). But once again, no countries stopped him – after all, he wasn't invading another nation, just moving soldiers around *within* his own, they thought! The same year, Hitler signed agreements with Italy and Japan – they agreed to stick up for each other if they were attacked.

By now though, Hitler's actions were starting to make world news. Many wondered what Hitler would do next.

In 1938, German troops marched into Austria, the country of Hitler's birth. Hitler had been threatening to invade Austria for years but the Austrian leader, a man named Kurt Schuschnigg, had worked hard to prevent it. Eventually, after Hitler moved his army close to Austria's border – and no other countries offered to help Austria – Schuschnigg resigned. The man who took his place as leader of Austria was a supporter of Hitler ... and invited him to take over! Whilst Schuschnigg was forced to clean toilets, the world began to realise that Hitler could soon be unstoppable. He had broken the Treaty of Versailles *again* and no country had stopped him.

▼ ***Source D*** *An Austrian girl gives a flower to an 'invading' German soldier, March 1938. Many Austrians wanted to be part of Germany and rejoiced when the Germans invaded. Austrians and Germans share a similar culture, customs, religion and language ... and Adolf Hitler was Austrian too! Note the swastika flags in the background – clearly the Austrians in this town were happy to see the Germans.*

WORK

1 What was the Treaty of Versailles?
2 Make a list of all the things Germany was <u>not</u> allowed to do according to the Treaty of Versailles.
3 Make another list showing all the ways Hitler broke the Treaty of Versailles up to 1938.
4 Why do you think other countries did nothing to stop Hitler's actions?

Hitler next turned his attention to the Sudetenland, a small area of Czechoslovakia that contained areas of people who spoke German as their first language (see **Source E**). Hitler told the world he wanted this region. Czechoslovakia wanted to keep it!

In September 1938, Neville Chamberlain, the British Prime Minister, tried to sort the problem out. He first visited the Czechoslovakian leader, Benes, who said Hitler could have the areas of the Sudetenland where most of the German speakers lived. Chamberlain, thinking this was quite fair, visited Hitler with the offer. But Hitler said he wanted *all* of the Sudetenland!

On 28 September, Chamberlain and several other leaders met Hitler once more. Benes wasn't even invited. An agreement was reached that said that Hitler could have all of the Sudetenland. Benes went along with this, hoping that Hitler would now leave his country alone. Hitler said he was happy with the outcome and the world breathed a sigh of relief. In Britain, Chamberlain was a hero – he had even got Hitler to sign a piece of paper saying he was satisfied with everything and didn't want anything else (see **Source G**).

▼ **Source F** *A French cartoon that appeared in newspapers on 28 September 1938 whilst the final meeting with Hitler in Munich was taking place. Chamberlain, Hitler, Deladier (the French leader) and Mussolini (Italy) are pictured in the 'dream cloud' at the top of the picture. In your opinion, what is the message of the cartoon?*

▲ **Source E** *A map of Europe in the 1930s showing Hitler's gradual takeover.*

▼ **Source G** *An adapted version of the Munich Agreement, signed by Chamberlain and Hitler on 30 September 1938.*

> We, Hitler and Chamberlain, have had a further meeting today and are in agreement that the question of British-German relations is very important.
>
> We regard the agreement signed last night [allowing Germany to have the Sudetenland] and the Anglo-German Naval Agreement [a deal in 1935 where Britain allowed Germany to have a bigger navy] as symbolic of the desire of our countries never to go to war with one another again.
>
> We are resolved that we shall use consultation to deal with any other questions that may concern our two countries and we are determined to continue our efforts to assure the peace of Europe.
>
> Neville Chamberlain   Adolf Hitler
>
> 30 September 1938

WISE UP WORDS

- Nazi-Soviet Pact   appeasement   rearmament   Lebensraum

Map labels: GERMANY (East Prussia), USSR, 1939 POLAND, CZECHOSLOVAKIA

But all Hitler's promises were exposed as lies in March 1939 when his soldiers took over the rest of Czechoslovakia. It seemed he wasn't satisfied with just the Sudetenland area – he wanted the whole country for living space! Suddenly, at last, the countries of Europe realised that Hitler could never be trusted and began preparing for war. They wondered if they would be next! Britain and France had each had enough of letting Hitler get away with things and agreed to help Poland if Hitler invaded.

Sure enough, Poland was next. Hitler threatened to invade in August 1939 but only after making a clever alliance with the USSR. He thought that the Russians might feel threatened if he continued to push his soldiers in their direction (see **Source E**) so he made a deal with Stalin, the Russian leader. This astounded Europe because Hitler had repeatedly said he hated the inferior Russians and their Communist rulers! However, the **Nazi-Soviet Pact**, as the deal was known, said the two countries wouldn't fight each other. A secret part of the deal said the Russians could have part of Poland if they let the Germans invade.

On 1 September 1939, German troops invaded Poland. Britain and France decided enough was enough. Two days later, on 3 September, Britain and France declared war on Germany. World War Two had started.

▼ **Source H** *Part of Chamberlain's radio speech to the nation when he announced that Britain was at war with Germany, 3 September 1939.*

> "This country is at war with Germany ... may God bless you all. It is evil things that we are fighting against — brute force, bad faith, injustice, oppression and persecution; and against that, I am certain that right will prevail."

FACT *Appeasement*

In the 1930s, many people were afraid of war. The horrors of the Great War were still fresh in people's memories. As a result, countries such as Britain and France decided to let aggressive leaders like Hitler have their own way rather than stand up to them. It was hoped that this course of action would avoid a large-scale war. This was called **appeasement** – trying to keep the peace through negotiation.

WORK

1 Match up the text on the left (list **A**) with the correct description on the right (list **B**).

List A	List B
Neville Chamberlain	Giving in to someone in order to avoid conflict
Appeasement	Taken over by Germany in March 1939
Sudetenland	Prime Minister of Britain during the late 1930s
3 September 1939	Area of Czechoslovakia given to Hitler in September 1938
Czechoslovakia	Date Britain and France declared war on Germany
Munich Agreement	Country invaded by Germany on 1 September 1939
Poland	Non-aggression deal signed by Britain and Germany

2 **a** What was the Nazi-Soviet Pact?
   b Why do you think people were surprised by it?

Germany at war

Topic Focus

➤ These pages will help you to understand why some Germans began to turn against Hitler and the Nazi Party.

Exam Focus

➤ Be able to describe how World War Two affected the German home front.

In the first few years of World War Two, the German army, navy and air force won one great battle after another. By the end of 1941, Hitler was beginning to call himself the 'Master of Europe'. A year before, he had attacked Denmark, Norway, Holland, Belgium, Luxembourg and France within a few weeks of each other. Soon all six countries had been defeated and occupied by the Germans.

The German people certainly felt the impact of the war – food and clothing had been **rationed** by November 1939 – but the news from the war zones was always good. In fact, the things Germany gained from victory – raw materials such as coal, oil, iron and captured land with huge factories and slave workers – made many Germans feel that Hitler was right when he said that war would make Germany very rich and powerful.

Then things began to go wrong!

Defeat

In 1941, Hitler's armies attacked the USSR (Soviet Russia). At first, German forces did well and got to within 60 miles of Russia's capital, Moscow. But a freezing Russian winter forced the Germans to stop. Their tanks wouldn't start, their guns wouldn't fire and their clothing wasn't warm enough. Soon, the huge Russian army began to push them back towards Germany. In one great battle at Stalingrad, over 80 000 Germans died and 90 000 surrendered. Only 5000 of them ever returned to Germany at the end of the war. There were defeats elsewhere too – British armies defeated them in North Africa and then America joined in on Britain and Russia's side! By the beginning of 1944, it was clear that Germany was doomed to defeat!

Hardship

The German people soon began to realise how difficult war was when they were not winning. Supplies were needed for the soldiers so sacrifices had to be made at home. There were severe food shortages (see **Source A**). The Nazis responded by asking the German people to commit themselves totally to winning the war (a policy named **Total War** by Goebbels). Everything was focused on making weapons, growing food and caring for wounded soldiers. Anything that didn't contribute to the war was stopped – beer houses, dance halls and even sweet shops were closed, letterboxes were boarded up and magazines were shut down. Factories were forced to stay open longer and even women were drafted in to work in them.

▼ **Source A** *Mathilde Wolff-Mönckeberg, living in Hamburg during the war, describes the problems her friend was having in 1943 after her husband went away to fight.*

"They have no children and she just can't manage without him. Rations for a single person are pathetic: 60 grammes of semolina and oats, 125 grammes of butter per week, one pound of meat and sausage per month. For this she has to queue for hours and there is no one at home in her icy flat to make her a meal. She has to face the rest of the day in frozen silence."

Bombing

From 1942, Britain and America began bombing German cities. Hitler had promised this would never happen. Night after night, major German cities were pounded by bomber planes and, not surprisingly, support for the Nazis began to weaken (see **Source B**).

▾ **Source B** *Mathilde Wolff-Mönckeberg in her diary.*

"How different the atmosphere is from that of the first war year when Nazi flags were flown, drums were beaten on the radio announcing victory. Since the defeat at Stalingrad and the start of Total War, all is grey and still. Everyone has been called up, even women up to 50 years old, and boys had to do anti-aircraft duties."

▸ **Source C** *A photograph of the German city of Dresden. Approximately 150 000 civilians died when Dresden was bombed in February 1945. Most of them burned to death in a huge firestorm that raged for two days after the bombing.*

TOP EXAM TIP

The war changed many people's views on the Nazis. Make sure you understand why.

▼ **Source D** *Bombs dropped on Germany and Britain, 1940–1945.*

YEAR	ON GERMANY	ON BRITAIN
1940	10 000	36 844
1941	30 000	21 858
1942	40 000	3260
1943	120 000	2298
1944	650 000	9151
1945	500 000	761

▼ **Source E** *Based on an eyewitness account in Hamburg on the morning after a heavy bombing raid.*

"Wednesday Morning

28 July 1943

There's no gas, no electricity, no water, no telephone and the lift doesn't work. It's hard to imagine the panic and chaos. There are no trams, no underground subway and no railway trains. Most people load some belongings on carts, bicycles, prams or carry things on their backs and walk just to get away, to escape. People who are wearing Nazi Party badges have them torn off their coats and there are screams of 'Let's get that murderer'. The police are doing nothing."

▼ **Source G** *The diary of Mathilde Wolff-Mönckeberg.*

"A thunderstorm of noise explodes above us. The house shakes, the windows tremble. For two hours, this ear-splitting terror goes on and all you can see is fire. We sat with wet towels over nose and mouth as the noise from one direct hit after another was such that plaster spilled from the walls and glass splintered from windows. I have never felt the nearness of death so intensely. The women and children are to be evacuated."

▶ **Source F** *Two Germans searching for food on a rubbish dump in Berlin, a dramatic example of how hungry ordinary Germans were in 1945.*

FACT *An invasion of Britain?*

Britain was on Hitler's hit list in 1940. His plan was to destroy all Britain's airports and fighter planes before launching an all-out invasion of troops across the English Channel from France. So a fierce air battle raged over England in the summer of 1940 – the Battle of Britain. By September, Britain had just managed to keep the German planes from destroying all their planes ... so Hitler gave up his plan to invade Britain and decided to bomb British cities and factories instead (known as the Blitz). He hoped to frighten Britain into surrender ... but he didn't!

▼ **Source H** *From a secret Nazi report, 1943.*

"A large section of the nation cannot imagine how the war will end and the telling of rude jokes against the state, even about the Führer himself, has increased."

WISE UP WORDS

• rationing   Total War

WORK

1 Test your understanding of these four pages by writing a sentence or two about the following words or phrases:

rationing • Stalingrad • Total War

2 Imagine you live in a large German city such as Dresden, Hamburg or Berlin during the war. Write three diary entries.

• **The first entry** should be written during the first few years of war. Write *why* the war is going well and what the mood of the nation is. Have there been any changes to daily life?

• **The second entry** should be made in the year after defeat at Stalingrad and the introduction of Total War. How has the defeat changed the mood of the nation and what does Total War mean to an ordinary German citizen?

• **Your final entry** should be made late in the war when conditions in Germany are very bad. How do people feel now about Hitler and the Nazis? What are the bombing raids like and what are they doing to civilian morale?

Did all Germans support the Nazis?

Topic Focus

▸ These pages will help you to understand why Hitler remained popular.

Many Germans admired Hitler and liked what the Nazis were doing. They supported them because of what they were achieving in Germany. Look at the four opinions below. They are based on quotes from German people who lived in Nazi Germany and summarise why Hitler and the Nazis remained popular.

Henry – factory worker

'I was one of six million out of work in 1933. Hitler said he would provide "work and bread" and he has kept his promise. I work long hours and get average wages but I have good working conditions and exciting leisure activities provided by the Strength through Joy movement.'

Walter – businessman

'Hitler has restored order to this country – crime and violence have all but disappeared. We needed strong leadership, someone who would stand up for Germany's interests after so many years at the bottom of the pile. Hitler has restored our pride in ourselves ... and when he decided to build up our armed forces, my friends and I made lots of money when our factories and businesses supplied goods to the army, navy and air force. Hitler banned trade unions so they can't make trouble and strike in our factories any more – and he forces lazy people to work, which saves the country millions in dole money – brilliant!'

Peter – 15-year-old schoolboy

'I love it in the Hitler Youth – the marching, the singing, throwing hand grenades and firing guns. The Hitler Youth summer camp I've just been on was my first ever holiday! Hitler means everything to me – he is like a mother and a father – he keeps me safe. I think Hitler is the best thing that has ever happened to Germany. He will restore our nation to its rightful position in the world.'

Hans – farmer

'The Nazis have made our lives more secure. The government buys our produce and gives us a guaranteed price for it. They have also stopped the banks from taking our land if we get into debt.'

However, not everyone supported what Hitler and the Nazis were doing. Hitler had very clear ideas about the kind of Germany he wanted – and some groups just didn't fit in. Women, for example, found their career opportunities very limited because Hitler felt women should concentrate on having babies and looking after their husbands! Many minorities too, like Jews and Gypsies, obviously opposed Hitler because they were so viciously persecuted. But thousands of ordinary Germans didn't fully support Hitler either. Some were uncomfortable with the new concentration camps and the dreaded Gestapo. Others were shocked at the treatment of the Jews ... or the Gypsies ... or the physically or mentally disabled. So how could ordinary Germans show their opposition to Hitler and the Nazis?

1. Grumbling

'Grumbling', or moaning as it is also known, was the lowest type of opposition to the Nazis. Often in the privacy of their own homes, people might tell an anti-Hitler joke or complain about the way their Jewish friends were being treated (see **Sources A** and **B**).

2. Passive resistance

This was when Germans publicly showed they didn't support the Nazis by refusing to do exactly as they were told. They may refuse to give the 'Heil Hitler' salute or refuse to give money to the Hitler Youth member as he went from house to house collecting funds (see **Source C**).

▼ **Source A** *From the BBC series* History File: Nazi Germany, *Episode Two.*

"The other week I go to a shop and say to the shopkeeper 'How's business?' – just small talk, stupid thing to say. His wife goes, 'Business – it's bad, it's non-existent!' We don't notice but another customer's come in. Yesterday I go back to the shop and say to the shopkeeper, 'How's your wife?' He says, 'They've taken her away for re-education – somebody heard her grumbling! She said business was bad so they turned her in!'

Maybe he thought it was me – in Germany today you trust no one."

▼ **Source B** *An anti-Nazi joke, popular in Germany in the 1930s.*

"Hitler was drowning in a lake when a young boy saved him. Hitler said, 'You've saved my life; how can I repay you?'

'Well', said the boy, 'I think I'd like an expensive funeral with a golden coffin and a magnificent marble gravestone'. Hitler was surprised. He said, 'Why do you want such a fantastic funeral? You're not going to die.'

'Oh no?' remarked the boy. 'Wait till I get home and tell my dad who I saved from drowning!'"

◄ **Source C** *As this photograph shows, not all Germans behaved exactly how the Nazis wanted. At this 1936 launch of a new battleship, can you find the shipyard worker who refused to give the 'Heil Hitler' salute?*

TOP EXAM TIP

An ordinary German's view on Hitler will depend on their circumstances. Make sure you understand that two different people, in different circumstances, will have different views and opinions.

3. Open opposition

Some Germans openly declared their dislike of Nazi ideas and policies. Some groups like the **White Rose** (see **Source D**) urged Germans to get rid of Hitler. They handed out anti-Nazi leaflets, put up posters and wrote graffiti on walls. Other groups blew up factories producing weapons or acted as spies and passed on military secrets to other countries (see **Source F**). The leaders of Germany's two main religious faiths – Protestants (40 million members) and Catholics (22 million) – made some criticism of the Nazis too (see **Source E**). For example, in 1941, the Catholic Church spoke out against Hitler's abuse of human rights, particularly the killing of physically and mentally disabled people.

▼ **Source D** *A leaflet against Hitler put out by a group known as the White Rose. Its leaders were brother and sister Hans and Sophie Scholl who were students at Munich University. They were caught in 1943 and beheaded for their 'crimes'. Just before she was executed, Sophie said, 'We have written and said what is in the minds of all of you – but you lack the courage to say it out loud.'*

A CALL TO ALL GERMANS

THIS WAR IS MOVING TO A CERTAIN END. HITLER CANNOT WIN IT – ONLY KEEP IT GOING ... BUT THE GERMAN PEOPLE SEES NOTHING AND DOES NOTHING. IN POLAND, 300 000 JEWS HAVE BEEN MURDERED. YOU KNOW OF THESE AND OTHER CRIMES ... WHY DO THE GERMAN PEOPLE DO NOTHING IN THE FACE OF THESE DREADFUL CRIMES?

THE WHITE ROSE

▼ **Source E** *This poem was written in prison by a German religious leader named Martin Niemoller. It explains why he felt he had unsuccessfully opposed the Nazis. In fact, Niemoller was one of only a few Church leaders who spoke out against Hitler's regime. Most claimed they were keeping religion and politics separate – they would leave Hitler alone if he left the Church alone. Even when Hitler started his National* **Reich Church** *(see fact box), few spoke out against him. Niemoller himself was arrested by the Gestapo in 1938 and kept in a concentration camp for seven years. Although orders were signed for his execution, the war ended just before it could be carried out.*

> First they came for the Jews –
> but I didn't speak out because I wasn't a Jew.
> Then they came for the Communists –
> but I didn't speak out because I wasn't a Communist.
> Then they came for the trade unionists –
> but I didn't speak out because I wasn't a trade unionist.
> Then they came for me –
> and there was no one left to speak up for me.

▼ **Source F** *A group of Edelweiss Pirates being hanged in 1944. There were approximately 2000 'pirate' groups all over Germany. They beat up Hitler Youth members, wrote graffiti on walls and distributed anti-Nazi leaflets. During the war, they helped crashed enemy airmen get back to Britain. As you can see, this opposition group in Cologne were executed for their resistance.*

▶ **Source G** *A photograph of the bombed-out remains of Hitler's map room in 1944. A group of high-ranking generals planned to kill Hitler and take over the country. Colonel Claus von Stauffenberg volunteered to plant a bomb under Hitler's map table but it was moved away from the Führer seconds before it was due to go off. The bomb failed to kill Hitler and the planned take-over failed. Stauffenberg and about 5000 others were executed in revenge for the attack.*

4. Kill Hitler

Hitler and the Nazis could not be voted out so one of the only ways to get rid of Hitler was to kill him. There *were* attempts on Hitler's life, but not many. A Jewish plot to kill him in 1935 failed. The closest any Germans got to assassination was in July 1944 when the war was going very badly. A group of army officers detonated a bomb under a table where Hitler was meeting other Nazi leaders. Despite killing four men, burning Hitler's hair, bursting his eardrums and blowing some of his clothes off – the Führer survived (see **Source G**)!

WISE UP WORDS

● Reich Church   White Rose

FACT *A new religion?*

Hitler hated Christianity (he wanted people to worship him ... and no one else!) but he didn't dare shut down all the churches because so many Germans were committed Christians. Instead, he said he'd leave them alone. But he didn't! He imprisoned any churchmen who made even a slight criticism of the Nazis and closed all church youth groups and church schools. He even set up a new Nazi church – the Reich Church – in an attempt to pull worshippers away from their traditional place of worship. In these new churches, only Nazis were allowed to preach, the Bible was banned (it was replaced by copies of *Mein Kampf*) and all crosses and religious objects were removed.

WORK

1 Look at the quotes of the four Germans on page 90. Using no more than 15 words for each person, summarise why they supported Hitler and the Nazis.

2 List as many different ways as possible that an ordinary German could show their opposition to Hitler and the Nazis. Your first example should be 'Telling an anti-Hitler joke' but you should be able to find at least five others.

CLASSIC EXAM QUESTION

Why was opposition to the Nazis so weak?

Auschwitz and the 'Final Solution'

Topic Focus

> These pages will help you to understand why the treatment of the Jews got worse as World War Two started.

Exam Focus

> You need to know why the Nazis decided to build death camps, and what role these camps played in the 'Final Solution'.

In early January 1942, a group of leading Nazis gathered at a large house in the elegant Berlin neighbourhood of Wannsee. They met to discuss the quickest and cheapest way to kill all the Jews left in Europe. This amounted to an estimated 11 million people! The Wannsee Conference, as the meeting became known, resulted in one of the most shocking plans ever devised – they decided to exterminate the entire Jewish population using poison gas.

Six major extermination or death camps dotted around Nazi-occupied Europe would carry out this 'Final Solution' to what the Nazis called their 'Jewish Problem'. Within a month, the first extermination camp was ready. It was just inside Poland, near the border with Germany, located near the Polish town of Oswiecim. The Germans called it Auschwitz … and it was to become the most famous death camp of all!

▼ **Source A** *Auschwitz extermination camp. Note the railway tracks. Thousands of Jews were brought to Auschwitz every week on cattle trucks. Train companies even charged the Nazi government for one-way tickets!*

For many years, Germany's Jews had been treated badly. But when war broke out in 1939, their treatment got worse – a lot worse! As Hitler's armies invaded more and more countries, more Jews became trapped under Nazi rule. Special murder squads called **Einsatzgruppen** (translated as 'One Sentence Groups') rounded up Jews in towns all over Europe. They would take them into the countryside and order them to dig a trench. The Jews were then shot and the trench became their mass grave. In some of the bigger cities, where there was a larger Jewish population, they were bricked into a separate section of the city, called a **ghetto**. Food, water and power were cut off resulting in hundreds of deaths every day.

> **FACT** *Hatred of Jews*
>
> Anti-Semitism is the official phrase for the discrimination of Jews. Anti-Semitism has been common in Europe for many centuries and at one time or another, Jews have been persecuted in nearly all European countries. Hitler's own violent anti-Semitism is a bit of a mystery. Even today, top historians are unsure as to why he hated Jews so much. Some argue that it could have something to do with his mother's death from breast cancer when he was a young man (she had a Jewish doctor) or his jealousy of the richer Jewish population in Vienna when he was living as a tramp.

◀ **Source B** *A photograph of Jews being rounded up after the Warsaw Ghetto Uprising in 1943, ready to be sent to Auschwitz. In April 1943, 750 Jews fought against German soldiers who were trying to clear the ghetto. The uprising lasted 43 days. Slowly, the German army crushed the resistance and 56 000 Jews were captured, most of whom had not had anything to do with the uprising. 7000 were shot, the rest sent to the nearest death camp – Auschwitz.*

But the Nazis regarded shooting (carried out by the Einsatzgruppen) and the ghettoes as an inefficient, slow method of killing. They needed a faster system, a way to kill thousands of people at once … so they created their death camps.

◀ **Source C** *An Einsatzgruppen soldier is watched by his colleagues as he murders a Jew in Poland, 1942.*

WORK

1 In your own words explain:
   i) final solution
   ii) Anti-semitism
2 What was the role of the Einsatzgruppen?
3 **a** What was the <u>role</u> of a ghetto?
   b Write a sentence or two about the Warsaw Ghetto Uprising.
   c Why do you think many Jews in camps and ghettoes decided not to fight against what was happening to them?

▼ **Source D** *From the Memoirs of Rudolf Höss, first commandant of Auschwitz. The Nazis tried to hide most of what was happening in the death camps, even going so far as banning leading Nazis from talking about it on the telephone and writing 'Final Solution' rather than 'extermination', 'special treatment' or 'killing by gas' in official letters.*

"I was suddenly summoned and Himmler [the man in charge of the 'Final Solution'] said:

'The Führer has ordered the Jewish question to be solved once and for all ... I have therefore earmarked [chosen] Auschwitz for this purpose. You will treat this order as absolutely secret, even from your superiors. The Jews are the sworn enemies of the German people and must be eradicated. Every Jew we can lay our hands on is to be destroyed now ... without exception.'"

During the first few months of 1942, Jews in every country where the Nazis ruled were taken from the ghettoes and put on trains. They were joined as prisoners by thousands of Gypsies, homosexuals, political opponents, the chronically sick and any other religious or minority group whom the Nazis considered unfit to live.

When they arrived at a death camp, the prisoners were immediately sorted into two groups by Nazi doctors: those who looked over 15 years old and were strong and healthy were sent to the left; the old, sick, pregnant women and mothers with young children were sent to the right. Those on the left (usually about 10–20%) were put to work, helping the camp guards murder the ones on the right. Any refusals to help would result in an immediate death sentence (see **Sources E** and **F**).

▼ **Source E** *Primo Levi, an Italian Jew, who survived his time at Auschwitz, explains how the Nazis tried to prevent panic amongst the 'chosen' victims.*

"The new arrivals did not know what awaited them. They were ... invited to undress 'for the showers'. Sometimes they were handed soap and towels and promised hot coffee after their showers. The gas chambers were, in fact, camouflaged as shower rooms with pipes, taps, dressing rooms, clothes hooks, benches and so forth."

▼ **Source F** *An eyewitness account by a death camp guard of what happened to those selected to die. He was giving evidence at a trial of Nazi war criminals at the end of the war.*

"A loudspeaker gave instructions: Strip ... hand all valuables and money in at the 'valuables' window. Women and young girls are to have their hair cut...

Stark naked, men, women and children passed by ... SS men pushed them into the gas chambers. Seven to eight hundred people in 93 square metres [the size of 2½ boxing rings]. All were dead after 32 minutes.

Jewish workers on the other side opened the wooden doors. They had been promised their lives in return for doing the horrible work ... the people were still standing like columns of stone, with no room to fall or lean. Even in death you could tell the families, all holding hands. It was difficult to separate them while emptying out the room for the next batch. The bodies were thrown out ... workers were busy checking mouths which they opened with iron hooks ... dentists knocked out gold teeth with hammers. The bodies were then burned."

▼ **Source G** *This pile of bodies was waiting to be burned as American soldiers arrived at the camp after Germany's defeat in 1945. Some soldiers were so shocked by what they saw, their hair turned white overnight. At one camp, US soldiers killed 300 camp guards who had not had time to run away – the surviving prisoners killed 200 more! At other camps, soldiers forced the local German population to walk past the unburned bodies, gas chambers and ovens to show them what had been going on so close to their homes.*

FACT *What name?*

The Nazis' attempt to wipe out the Jewish race is commonly known as the **Holocaust**. However, in recent years, some Jews have objected to this word as it means 'sacrifice'. They argue that this implies that Jews were 'offering themselves' in some way. The word 'churban', which means 'destruction', is therefore preferred by some or 'genocide', which means the deliberate extermination of a race of people.

▼ **_Source H_** *Fritz Stangl, the man in charge of Treblinka extermination camp. The camps were run by a branch of the SS called Death's Head Units (they wore a skull and cross bones on their uniforms).*

> "Cargo. They were cargo … I remember the pits full of blue-black corpses … a mass of rotting flesh. Wirth [a senior SS official] said, 'What shall we do with this garbage?' I think that started the thinking of them as cargo."

FACT *Fighting back!*

Some Jews did fight against what was happening to them. The Warsaw Ghetto Uprising against the German soldiers controlling the ghetto lasted 43 days. There were also rebellions at the camps. In Treblinka, in 1943, 150 prisoners managed to escape, killing 15 camp guards in the process. However, the Nazis soon regained control and all of the escapees were killed. 550 other prisoners were killed in revenge too!

FACT *Who knew?*

150 German companies used Auschwitz prisoners as slaves to build their goods. Other firms competed for the contract to design and build the gas chambers and ovens in which people were murdered and burned. In 1943, a newspaper in one of Germany's largest cities even carried the headline 'Jews to be exterminated'.

Thousands of people, not just loyal Nazis, helped with the 'Final Solution' – ordinary people like railway workers all around Germany who loaded Jews onto cattle trucks bound for the camps, office clerks, typists, telephone operators, policemen and soldiers.

Governments in other countries, like the USA and Britain, knew something terrible was happening too, but not the scale of it. Could they have bombed the railway lines or camps? What do you think?

By the end of the war, over six million people, mainly Jews, had been murdered in death camps like Auschwitz. It has been estimated that, on average, 4000 people were murdered every day for four years in these camps.

WISE UP WORDS

• ghetto Holocaust Einsatzgruppen

▼ **_Source I_** *A map of Europe showing the main concentration and extermination camps. Concentration camps tended to be more like prisons where inmates were put to work in terrible conditions. They were often worked to death. Extermination camps were slightly different – their only purpose was to kill.*

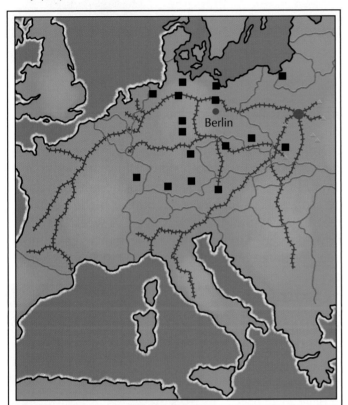

▲	Extermination camps	
■	Concentration camps	
⊢┼┼⊣	Transport routes (rail)	

Country	Number of Jews killed	%
Poland	3 000 000	90
Germany	210 000	90
Czechoslovakia	155 000	86
Holland	105 000	75
Hungary	450 000	75
Ukraine	900 000	60
Romania	300 000	50
Russia	107 000	11

WORK

1 Look at **Source D**.

   a In what way was the Final Solution different from the way the Nazis had treated Jews since 1933?

   b Why do you think the Nazis tried to keep the specific details about the killings secret from the German people?

2 **a** In your own words, explain what happened to prisoners upon arrival at Auschwitz.

   b Why do you think Jews were told they were going for a shower?

3 The following list of people all helped to make the Final Solution happen. The list is in no particular order.

   • Police and soldiers who rounded up the Jews for transportation and guarded the ghettoes.

   • Leading Nazis such as Himmler and Heydrich (he was in charge of the Einsatzgruppen).

   • Camp Commandants such as Höss (see **Source D**) and Stangl (see **Source H**).

   • Hitler.

   • The governments of foreign countries, including Britain, who did nothing to stop it.

   • Guards who worked in the camps.

   • Engineers who designed the camps and built the gas chambers.

   • Train drivers who drove the trains to the camps.

   • The German public who did nothing to stop it.

   • Office workers, typists and telephone operators who worked in the camps or organised the lists of Jews' names.

   • Nazi doctors and dentists who helped with selection and handling of the dead (see **Source F**).

   i) Arrange the list in order of responsibility. Put the person (or people) who, in your opinion, was (or were) most responsible for the Holocaust at the top of your list right down to the person (or people) with least responsibility at the bottom.

   ii) Compare your list with someone else in your class. To what extent do you agree or disagree?

   iii) Who is most to blame and why?

   iv) Who is least to blame? Give reasons as to why you've placed them at the bottom of your list.

   v) Who on your list could have realistically stopped the Holocaust?

How did Hitler die?

Exam Focus
> Make sure you can explain why Hitler committed suicide in April 1945.

In April 1945, British and American soldiers were moving towards Berlin (Germany's capital city) from the west and the Russian army was advancing on Berlin from the east. The German army was being beaten. Food supplies in the city were decreasing day by day. Ordinary civilians took to scavenging food from rubbish tips or eating stray cats and dogs. With allied soldiers closing in on both sides, Hitler ordered that in Berlin, 'every building, every house, every floor and every hedge must be defended to the last man and the last bullet'. Hitler and his closest followers retreated to a special underground bunker made from reinforced concrete and steel, deep below the city streets. By 30 April, Hitler was dead. A week later, Germany surrendered and the war was over. But how did Hitler die? Study the following sources carefully and try to establish how Adolf Hitler, one of the most infamous men in history, spent the last few days of his life.

▼ **Source A** *Ulrich de Maiziere, a German army officer who spent time with Hitler in April 1945.*

"Hitler was a very sick man. His right arm shook badly and he dragged his feet when he walked. He wore blue glasses to protect his eyes. He had very poor eyesight and everything had to be written in large letters. He was clearly mentally ill but he seemed to have lost none of his special power to inspire loyalty and dedication."

▼ **Source B** *Written in 1966 by Albert Speer, Hitler's chief architect who spent time with Hitler in his bunker in 1945.*

"He was shrivelling up like an old man. His limbs trembled and he walked stooped. Even his voice shook and then broke when he got excited. His face was pale and swollen; his uniform, which in the past he had kept very neat, was now stained with food he had eaten with a shaking hand."

▶ **Source C** *The last photograph of Adolf Hitler, taken on his 56th birthday (20 April 1945), as he presents medals to Hitler Youth boys who he has ordered to defend Berlin.*

▼ **Source D** *From a modern history textbook.*

"In April 1945, the Russian army entered Berlin. Hitler at last realised what his generals had known a year before – Germany could not win the war. But rather than surrender, he decided to commit suicide.

Living with him in the bunker were Goebbels and his family, and Eva Braun, a woman who had loved him for many years and who now wanted to die with him. On 29 April, they were married. Early the next morning, Hitler shot himself and Eva took poison. Their bodies were then carried into a small garden above the bunker, soaked with petrol and burned. The day after that, Goebbels and his wife also took their lives after having their six children poisoned."

Source E *Alan Bullock, a top historian.*

"Hitler was lying on the sofa, which was soaked in blood; he had shot himself through the mouth. On his right side lay Eva Braun, Hitler's wife, also dead; she had swallowed poison. The time was 3:30pm on the afternoon of Monday 30 April 1945, ten days after Hitler's 56th birthday. The bodies were laid in a shallow depression of sandy soil close to the porch. Picking up the five cans of petrol, Hitler's SS adjutant [assistant] poured the contents over the two corpses and set fire to them with a lighted rag."

Source F *This photograph was circulated by the Russian army shortly after Hitler's death. Many at the time thought it was Adolf Hitler. However, the photograph was soon exposed as a fake – it wasn't Hitler at all but an unfortunate body double.*

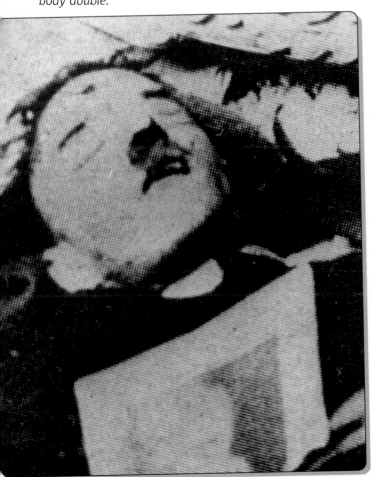

FACT *Pass the ashtray please!*

The Russian army found Hitler's body and took part of his skull back to Moscow. Dental records proved it was Hitler's skull. There was a 7.65mm bullet hole through the temple and traces of cyanide in the bone tissue (did Hitler swallow a poisoned pill at the same time as he shot himself?). The skull fragments remain in Moscow to this day, occasionally appearing for exhibitions. Apparently, part of the skull was presented to Stalin, Russia's leader during the war, who used it as an ashtray for five years before returning it to the State Archive.

WORK

1 Look at **Sources A** and **B**.
   a In your own words, describe the condition of Adolf Hitler in April 1945.
   b Rewrite either **Source A** or **Source B**, pretending you work for Joseph Goebbels, Head of Propaganda.

2 Look at **Sources D** and **E**.
   a Who was Eva Braun?
   b According to the sources, how did Hitler die?
   c The people who wrote **Sources D** and **E** were not there when Mr and Mrs Hitler committed suicide. How do you think they've gone about finding out what happened?
   d What happened to Hitler's body after his suicide?

3 Look at **Source F**.
   a Why do you think Hitler felt it necessary to have a 'body double'?
   b Why do you think the Russians took this photograph, quickly printed it all over Russia and sent it to nearly all fighting countries?

Have <u>you</u> been learning?

TASK 1 Cartoon time

Study this cartoon carefully. It appeared in the *London Evening Standard* in 1936.

a Who is the figure walking over the large group of men? Where is the man heading?

b What is the man doing with his hands and what does this gesture usually mean?

c Why do you think the cartoonist has used the word 'spineless' to describe the various leaders of different countries? What does this insult usually mean?

d According to the cartoon, how can the leaders of democracy stop Hitler from walking all over them?

TASK 2 Reputation

The following 12 facts about Hitler and Nazi Germany are all true:

1 Hitler came to power legally.

2 Hitler was very popular with most Germans who appreciated his efforts to restore Germany to its former glory.

3 Nazi Germany was a racist state where terrible persecution took place on a daily basis.

4 Millions of Jews were murdered as part of the Nazis' 'Final Solution'.

5 German scientists made huge technological advances during the Nazi period, for example, in rocket science and synthetic (man-made) fibre technology.

6 Thousands of 'undesirables', such as beggars, Gypsies, mentally and physically disabled people and homosexuals, were killed because they 'polluted' Nazi Germany.

7 During Hitler's time as Führer, he nearly wiped out unemployment. It dropped from six million in 1933 to under half a million by 1938.

8 Hitler ended democracy in Germany. As dictator, he allowed no opposition and used propaganda and terror to control people. Hitler once said, 'Terror is the best political weapon. Nothing drives people harder than a fear of sudden death'.

9 The Nazis created the first motorway system in the world. By the end of the 1930s, motorways linked all parts of Germany together.

10 Hitler invaded several countries in Europe, which led to the start of World War Two. Up to 50 million people died in the war.

11 Nazi doctors carried out terrible medical experiments, such as removing vital organs from victims without using anaesthetic to see how long they could survive without them.

12 Right up to the start of World War Two, many top European politicians admired Hitler. Many thought that the spread of Communism from Russia was a greater threat to world peace than Hitler – and Hitler said he was going to destroy Communism. One British journalist wrote in 1937, 'The Nazis have brought order, political peace, more work, better living conditions and the promise to make Germany a great nation once more. The day may come when Britain will thank God that Germany has a strong army to defend Europe against Communist Russia.'

a Sort the 12 facts into two groups. **Group 1** should contain all the positive things about Hitler and the Nazis. **Group 2** should contain all the negative things.

b Write two paragraphs based on each list. One should be called 'Hitler and the Nazis: saviours of Germany'. The other should be called 'Hitler and the Nazis: evil men doing evil things.'

c What is your own opinion of Hitler and the Nazis? Write a paragraph called 'Hitler's reputation: my opinion'.

TASK 3 Question time

Look at these genuine GCSE questions carefully. Why not try to complete one, two or even all of them as a revision exercise? In brackets after each question, you will find the pages of this book where there is information that might refresh your memory.

- What was Hitler's attitude to the Treaty of Versailles? (pages 82–85)
- How did Hitler's attitude to the Treaty of Versailles affect his foreign policy? (pages 82–85)
- Why did Hitler take over the Sudetenland? (pages 82–85)
- Why did Hitler invade Austria? (pages 82–85)
- Why did German armies invade Poland in September 1939? (pages 82–85)
- How did Hitler deal with opposition to Nazi rule? (pages 44–45 and 90–93)
- Why did different groups oppose Nazi rule? (pages 90–93)
- How did some young people oppose Nazi policies between 1933 and 1945? (pages 62–63 and 90–93)
- How effective was Nazi control over Germany from 1933 to 1945? (pages 82–95)

TASK 4 War crimes

After the war, many Nazis were put on trial and executed for their part in the Holocaust. They were called 'war criminals'. Adolf Eichmann was one of the best-known war criminals because he was captured by the Americans immediately after the war but managed to escape to South America using a false name.

He was wanted for trial because he organised for Jews to be sent to death camps. He was at the Wannsee Conference (January 1942) where plans for the 'Final Solution' were worked out and took an active part in planning dates and train times for Jews to be taken away and murdered.

In 1960, he was kidnapped from his home in Argentina by Israeli soldiers and put on trial in Jerusalem (Israel had been set up after the war as an independent Jewish nation). He was found guilty and hanged in 1962.

◄ **Source A**
Eichmann on trial in Jerusalem 1962.

▼ **Source B** *Eichmann, speaking at his trial.*

'I am covered in guilt, I know that. But I had nothing to do with killing Jews. I've never killed a Jew and I've never ordered anyone to kill a Jew.'

a Is it true that Eichmann never personally killed Jews? Look back at his involvement in the Final Solution. Was he right when he said: i) 'I've never killed a Jew'; ii) 'I've never ordered anyone to kill a Jew'?

b If you were responsible for prosecuting Eichmann in 1962, what would you charge him with? Remember, you must be able to prove the charges.

c Other war criminals escaped after the war and have never been found. Do you think we should continue to hunt for these people (they would be very old by now), or let the matter drop?

What do I revise?

The study of Germany between 1918 and 1945 is one of the most fascinating areas in history...and it is certainly very detailed – and often complicated! At first it may seem like you have a near impossible amount to revise, but don't stress too much about this – you won't be expected to know every intricate detail, date, event and person connected in any way to German history during the inter-war years. You are a History *student* after all (not a History professor or college lecturer), but you must endeavour to understand the following four key areas in order to get the highest mark possible in your examination.

1 Have a basic knowledge of these key areas:

a The impact of the Great War on Germany ... and the Peace Treaty that followed!

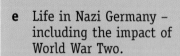

b The highs and lows of the Weimar Republic.

c The early years of Hitler and the Nazi Party.

d Hitler's rise to power and his take over of Germany.

e Life in Nazi Germany – including the impact of World War Two.

Those students looking for higher grades will be looking for links between the key areas too. For example, a thorough understanding of Hitler's ascent to power can only be achieved if the student understands the weaknesses of the Weimar Republic.

2 Know about the key individuals who have influenced Germany's history between the wars.

Try to learn a little about their lives, their beliefs and their influences, their impact on Germany and their roles in its history between 1919 and 1945. For example, why not prepare 'pen portraits' or 'mini biographies' on:

- Kaiser Wilhelm ll

- Friedrich Ebert

- Gustav Stresemann

- Adolf Hitler

- Joseph Goebbels

- Heinrich Himmler

3

Night of the Long Knives

Kristallnacht

Spartacus Revolt

Be able to write a short description of key events. You should be able to explain why the event occurred and describe the impact and consequences of the event.

Munich Beer Hall Putsch

Kapp Putsch

4 When you are comfortable with your knowledge and understanding of key areas, individuals and events, work hard on some of the 'big questions' that a student who is looking for some of the higher grades must know. For example:

- Was the Weimar Republic doomed from the start?

- How successful was the Nazi Party in winning the support of the German people?

- Why did the Germans allow Hitler to take power?

- Why did some Germans oppose the Nazis?

Getting your revision right

Most people experience exam nerves ... so it is perfectly natural to feel anxious when exam time approaches. But whilst a certain amount of exam stress can be used to motivate you to revise properly, it is important to keep on top of exam anxiety ... and the best way to do this is to be ORGANISED!

Before you start

Planning – Be organised, make a realistic plan you can stick to and STICK TO IT!

Be realistic – do not attempt to revise for more than 30–45 minutes at a time – break up your revision with breaks and rewards. If you give yourself a 10 minute break between two 30–45 minute sessions you will be amazed how much more you'll get done!

Support – Find a 'revision buddy' to revise with and to test you, it is often a big help.

Organise yourself – Sort out your revision environment that you are going to work in. Make sure you have everything you need – your revision books, pens, paper, stick-it notes, index cards etc. Make sure it's a quiet place where you are comfortable. Divide your work, folder or revision notes into sections that are easy to use, ordered and well structured.

Believe in yourself – You wouldn't have been given a place on the course if you didn't have the ability to do it. Therefore, if you prepare for the exams properly you should do fine, and meet your target level if not exceed it.

Keep things in perspective – The exams might seem like the most crucial thing right now, but in the grander scheme of your whole life they are only a small part.

Top tips

Create an overview of what you want to revise and break each subject down into manageable chunks. Make headings and allocate each section on a monthly or weekly planner.

Set definite start and finish times for your revision sessions and have a clear goal for each session.

Build a system of regular review into your revision, checking what you know and what you don't know.

Ask your teachers for practice questions or past papers.

Practise making plans and answering questions under timed conditions.

During breaks do something completely different – listen to music, have a chocolate biscuit, make a cup of tea for example.

Use Mind Maps (see pages 78–79) for complicated topics. Use pictures and symbols that spring to your mind.

You should know how best you learn. Are you an auditory, visual or kinaesthetic learner? Make sure you use this information to help your revision.

On the big day

Don't work all through the night, get an early night instead.

Make sure you know where and when the exam is and leave plenty of time to get there.

Make sure you have all your equipment in advance ... and spare pens!

Avoid too much nicotine and caffeine. Water is best – if you are 5% dehydrated, then your concentration drops 20%.

Don't listen to people who might try to wind you up about what might come up in the exam – they don't know any more than you!

And finally, when you come out of your exam don't listen to what other people tell you *they* have written, they might not be right. This could knock your confidence, especially if you have another paper to go!

Give 'em what they want!

Your guide to understanding how to answer different types of questions

GCSE History courses require you to learn tons of fascinating facts, loads of interesting stories, dozens of famous names and lots of key dates. Your teacher will work incredibly hard to help you work on ways to remember as much of this as you can. But a GCSE History course is not just about filling your head with all this knowledge ... you actually have to sit an exam or two as well! But the exam is not simply designed to test what you can remember, it is aimed at testing your skills as a historian too. As a result, the exam questions themselves, and the way they are worded, are designed to test these skills. So it is vital that you understand exactly what each type of question requires you to write in order to get the best marks possible. Look carefully through the list of key words that most commonly appear in exam questions. Remember, giving the examiner what they want is one of your keys to success.

State...

Write the main points briefly.

Define...

Give the meaning.

Summarise...

Bring together the main points into a short, sharp paragraph or two.

Contrast...

Look for differences.

Compare...

Are the things very similar (alike) or are there important differences? You might be asked which is best, and why?

Outline...

Choose the most important parts or aspects of a topic. Generally speaking, ignore the minor detail and concentrate on the 'bigger' points.

Justify...

Write down the main reasons to support an argument or action.

Discuss...

Write about the important aspects of the topic. Think whether there are two sides to the question or argument and consider both sides.

Describe...

This means you have to write in detail about the event, situation or discovery for example. Write down lots of key facts.

Evaluate...

Use your knowledge or the information in front of you to judge the importance or success of something.

Explain why...

Make something very clear, giving lots of detail.

Now you are familiar with the different types of questions – and what they demand of you – why not practice writing answers for some of the following questions.

- Describe the problems the Weimar Republic faced in the early 1920s.
- Summarise how Hitler became Chancellor in 1933?
- 'Propaganda was the most important reason for the lack of opposition in Nazi Germany'. Do you agree with this statement? Explain your answers carefully.
- Outline the main features of the education of children in Nazi Germany?
- Explain why opposition to the Nazis was so weak?

Glossary

Abdicate   To give up the throne of a country.

Appeasement   The policy of giving someone what they want in the hope that their demands will stop.

Article 48   The part of the Weimar Constitution that gave the president 'emergency powers' to act without getting the support of the Reichstag in times of crisis.

Aryan   A person of German or Scandinavian origin, usually fair-haired and blue eyed. The Nazis believed that Aryans were superior to all other races.

Communism   A political system where all property is owned by the government; people are equal and they are paid by the government according to their needs.

Communist   A person who lives in a country where the government follows the political system known as Communism.

Concentration camp   A harsh camp for civilian prisoners.

Conscription   A law making all men of a certain age join the armed forces and be available to fight at any time.

Constitution   The rules by which a country is governed.

Dawes Plan   An agreement between the USA and European countries in 1924 (drawn up in America by Charles Dawes). The plan organised for US loans to be given to European countries, especially Germany, in order for them to build factories, roads and so on.

Demagogue   Someone who can rouse people by appealing to their passions and prejudices.

Demilitarised zone (DMZ)   An area where no soldiers (or military equipment) are allowed to go.

Democratic republic   A system of running a country in which all adults have the right to vote for the government they want.

Dictator   A ruler with total control over how a country is governed.

Diktat   The nickname given to the hated Treaty of Versailles. Translates as 'dictated peace'.

Edelweiss Pirates   One of the many groups of working-class youngsters who refused to join the Hitler Youth and formed their own street gangs.

Einsatzgruppen   Special death squads that hunted Jews and other 'undesirables' in the countries invaded by Nazi Germany.

Enabling Law   A law passed in 1933 giving Hitler the power to act without consulting the Reichstag or the President.

Eugenics   The study of methods of improving the human race.

Euthanasia   The act of killing someone painlessly. Sometimes called 'mercy killing'.

Final Solution   The Nazi name given to the attempt to wipe out Europe's Jews between 1942 and 1945.

Free Corps   A group of ex-soldiers in Germany who joined with the Government in 1919 to fight the Spartacus League (Communists).

Führer   German word for leader, used by Hitler as leader of Nazi Germany.

Gauleiters   Loyal members of the Nazi Party responsible for 'controlling' an area of a large German city.

German Labour Front   An organisation set up by the Nazis to improve the lives of workers. It replaced all trade unions.

Gestapo   The secret police under Nazi rule.

Ghetto   An area where members of a particular racial group are forced (or choose) to live.

Hereditary   Passed on genetically from one generation to another.

Hitler Youth Organisation   A Nazi youth movement set up to replace all other youth groups.

Holocaust   Usually used to describe the murder of millions of Jews by the Nazis during World War Two.

Hyperinflation   A sudden, dramatic rise in prices.

Indoctrinate   Another word for 'brainwash' – to teach someone to accept a belief without question.

Infamous   Well known for something bad.

Inferior   Of lower quality, position or status.

Kapp Putsch   The violent attempt to take over Germany in 1920, led by Wolfgang Kapp.

Kellogg-Briand Pact   A 1928 deal signed by 65 countries promising not to attack each other.

Kristallnacht   Night of Broken Glass in November 1938 when Jews and their shops and businesses were attacked all over Germany.

League of Nations   An international peacekeeping organisation set up at the end of the Great War.

Lebensborn   Maternity homes where unmarried women could go to and hope to get pregnant by a 'racially pure' SS soldier.

Lebensraum   Living space. The Nazis believed that the German people needed and deserved more land.

Left wing   Believing in (or a belief in) ideas closely associated with Communism.

Locarno Pact   A deal signed in 1925 between Germany, Britain, France, Belgium and Italy where they promised not to invade each other.

Looting   The theft of goods during a war.

Majority   The greater proportion.

Mass rally   A huge meeting.

Mein Kampf   A book written by Hitler containing his views.

Mutiny   A rebellion by soldiers and sailors who refuse to take orders.

National Labour Service   An organisation that arranged compulsory work (planting trees, building roads and so on) for all male 18 to 25 year olds.

Nazi-Soviet Pact   A 1939 deal between Germany and Soviet Russia that said that both countries would not fight against each other. A secret part of the deal agreed to split Poland between them if (and when) Germany invaded.

Night of the Long Knives   The name given to the night when the leaders of the SA were killed in 1934 after Hitler had decided they were a threat to his power. The SA continued but was reduced in importance.

Nuremberg Laws   Laws passed in 1935 that banned Jews from many areas of German life.

Pacifist   A person who refuses on principle to take part in war.

Passive resistance   To protect against government, law and so on by non-violent acts.

Persecute   Treat someone cruelly because of race, religion and so on.

Propaganda   Information that is spread by a government to influence people's opinions.

Proportional Representation   A system of elections in which the number of politicians elected for a particular party is in proportion to the number of votes the party receives. PR can lead to lots of small parties gaining seats and an instable government.

Putsch   An attempt to seize power using violence.

Rationing   Giving every person a fixed amount of certain sorts of food, fuel or clothing when they are in short supply.

Rearmament   Building up new stocks of weapons or replacing old weapons with new ones.

Reich Church   A new Church set up by the Nazis in an attempt to pull worshippers away from traditional places of worship.

Reichstag   The German parliament.

Reparations   Payments made by Germany to the winning nations after the Great War to compensate for the damage done.

Republic   A country where there is no king or queen and the head of state is called a President.

Self-sufficient   When a country is able to provide for itself without having to trade with others for supplies.

Spartacus League   Communist Party in Germany who wanted a revolution similar to the one that had taken place in Russia in 1917.

SS   Elite group of 'racially pure' Aryan soldiers who were totally loyal to Hitler. Stands for Schutz Staffel, which means 'Protection Squad' as they were originally set up as Hitler's private blackshirted bodyguards.

Sterilisation   The process of making a person unable to have children.

Strength through Joy   Kraft durch Freude, an organisation that offered leisure activities to hardworking Germans.

Sturm Abteilung   The official title for Hitler's private army of brownshirted thugs that he employed to beat up opponents and guard early Nazi meetings.

Superior   Of higher quality, position or status.

Swastika   The crooked cross symbol adopted by the Nazi Party as their emblem.

Swing types   Richer youngsters who rebelled against the Nazis by listening to banned music and reading banned books.

Synagogue   Jewish place of worship and religious instruction.

Three Ks   Kinder, Kirche, Kuche (children, church and cooking). The Nazis hoped all women's lives would be dominated by these three things.

Total War   A phrase introduced by Goebbels during World War Two. He called for all Germans, civilians and soldiers to take an active part in the war.

Treaty of Versailles   An agreement that the German government signed at the end of the Great War which outlined Germany's punishments.

Volkswagen   Translates as People's (Volks) Car (Wagen). Hitler promised to produce a car that ordinary people could afford, so got Ferdinand Porsche to design the now famous 'Beetle'.

Weimar Republic   The name given to Germany's democratic system between 1919 and 1933.

White Rose   An anti-Nazi youth group.

Young Plan   An agreement made in 1929 between Germany and the countries they owed money to after the Great War. Reparation payments were reduced and Germany was allowed longer to pay.

Index